HBR Guide to
Changing
Your Career

Harvard Business Review Guides

Arm yourself with the advice you need to succeed on the job, from the most trusted brand in business. Packed with how-to essentials from leading experts, the HBR Guides provide smart answers to your most pressing work challenges.

The titles include:

HBR Guide to Being More Productive

HBR Guide to Better Business Writing

HBR Guide to Building Your Business Case

HBR Guide to Buying a Small Business

HBR Guide to Coaching Employees

HBR Guide to Data Analytics Basics for Managers

HBR Guide to Delivering Effective Feedback

HBR Guide to Emotional Intelligence

HBR Guide to Finance Basics for Managers

HBR Guide to Getting the Right Work Done

HBR Guide to Leading Teams

HBR Guide to Making Every Meeting Matter

HBR Guide to Managing Stress at Work

HBR Guide to Managing Up and Across

HBR Guide to Negotiating

HBR Guide to Office Politics

HBR Guide to Performance Management

HBR Guide to Persuasive Presentations

HBR Guide to Project Management

HBR Guide to
Changing Your Career

HARVARD BUSINESS REVIEW PRESS

Boston, Massachusetts

Copyright 2018 Harvard Business School Publishing Corporation

All rights reserved

Printed in the United States of America

10 9 8 7 6 5 4 3 2 1

No part of this publication may be reproduced, stored in or introduced into a retrieval system, or transmitted, in any form, or by any means (electronic, mechanical, photocopying, recording, or otherwise), without the prior permission of the publisher. Requests for permission should be directed to permissions@hbsp.harvard.edu, or mailed to Permissions, Harvard Business School Publishing, 60 Harvard Way, Boston, Massachusetts 02163.

The web addresses referenced in this book were live and correct at the time of the book's publication but may be subject to change.

Library of Congress Cataloging-in-Publication Data

Title: HBR guide to changing your career.
Other titles: Harvard Business Review guide to changing your career |
    Changing your career | Harvard business review guides.
Description: Boston, Massachusetts : Harvard Business Review Press, [2018] |
    Series: Harvard business review guides | Includes index.
Identifiers: LCCN 2018002104 | ISBN 9781633693104 (pbk. : alk. paper)
Subjects: LCSH: Career changes. | Mid-career.
Classification: LCC HF5384 .H39 2018 | DDC 650.14--dc23 LC record available at https://lccn.loc.gov/2018002104

ISBN: 9781633693104

eISBN: 9781633693111

The paper used in this publication meets the requirements of the American National Standard for Permanence of Paper for Publications and Documents in Libraries and Archives Z39.48-1992

MIX
Paper from
responsible sources
FSC
www.fsc.org
FSC® C132124

What You'll Learn

You're well into your career, and yet you're not where you want to be. Perhaps you've done everything you need to do to be named a partner, but your firm has encountered a crisis that's put all promotions on hold. Maybe a hobby or side gig has helped unearth a new passion you'd love to pursue full time. Perhaps you've come to realize that your current role is no longer meaningful. Or maybe you've exceeded all of the goals you set for your current career and you're ready for a new challenge. How do you envision possible new professional selves, explore your options, and embark on a dramatic career makeover when you have a mortgage to pay, kids to support, college and retirement funds to feed—and a full life and full-time job? Can you really set aside the years you've invested in your education and current industry? How can you make a radical change when there are so many demands on you?

Whether you know what you want your second act to be or you have no clue—only that what you're doing isn't a match—this guide will help you chart a course and make the switch. You'll discover how to:

- Break free of what your career is now to consider what it could be

- Get an accurate picture of the skills and abilities you bring to the table

- Create experiments that won't sabotage your current job

- Assess the financial implications of making a change

- Develop a compelling way to tell your story—tying even seemingly unrelated jobs into a cohesive narrative

- Build expertise in a new field

- Land a new role

Contents

Contents

SECTION THREE

Is Career Change Right for You?

SECTION FOUR

Get Going

Contents

SECTION FIVE

Get Inspired

Introduction

Transformation. Second act. Stuck. Reinvention. Cross-roads. Pivot. Do-over. Considering a career change can be a gnarly swirl of exhilaration and trepidation. Whether you're coming from a place of restless stagnation born of security or one of desperation—you cannot take another day of doing what you're doing—you want a change.

Career change could be something you've daydreamed about for a while, or maybe it's a boiling point that you've just hit, but it probably feels a bit out of reach. You've invested a lot of education, time, and energy in your current job. You're the go-to person for people at work, a topic or process expert. You're not a failure by any stretch of the imagination; you're just longing for something different.

The conventional wisdom for changing careers is to follow a measured and thoughtful path. Assess your strengths, imagine possible selves, craft small (and safe!)

experiments, evaluate the outcome of those exercises, and chart a new course taking into account all of that information and experience. But this approach can lead to analysis paralysis. How can you stop reflecting and start *doing*? This guide will help you do just that.

Who This Book Is For

This is not a book for first-time job seekers or recent grads. Rather, it's for you if you've been out in the workforce for at least a few years. It's for you if your first "real" job didn't turn out the way you'd hoped. It's for you if you're well into your career (or even into your second career). This collection is for people with a complicated context: You have an advanced degree, and the student loans to prove it. You have a family that anticipates an annual holiday to relax and reconnect. You have a network that enjoys trading favors and tapping your expertise. And you have direct reports who are counting on you to help shepherd them up the ladder at work.

But a complicated context doesn't mean you're trapped. There are benefits to having held at least one career. You have experience. You have a network. You've faced a crisis or two and survived—even learned something. You know what you like and what you don't like. You know how you prefer to work and something about which type of culture or work environment you do best in. You understand the distinction between being good at something and enjoying what you're doing.

If you know exactly what you want your next career to be—you just haven't figured out how to cross over—this book is for you. Maybe you don't know what you want to do next—just that the current situation isn't the right fit. The content in this volume will help you see how even sifting through the long list of things you don't enjoy and wouldn't want to pursue can help you narrow the field to find something that would interest you.

You can take that knowledge and close the gap between dreaming of something else and actually doing something else. Change, especially for something as deeply held as your work identity, can feel scary. But it's an enormous opportunity for discovery and growth. We all have numerous possible selves. What would our lives look like if we took a different path? What's a safe way to test a new direction? This guide will give you questions to reflect on what you want, stories to inspire you, and tools to help you take action.

How to Use This Book

Just as there's no one track for any of us to follow in our careers, there's no one way to read this book. Some of you will want to read it cover to cover, craft a detailed transition plan, set milestones, and start ticking through items. Others will dive into the section that speaks to them. If you feel despair because it seems like a significant change can never happen, the success stories in the Get Inspired section will motivate you to work through the challenging, more self-reflective sections of the book. Some of you may dip your toes in by trying some of the experiments in the Get Going section. Others may read the chapter on job crafting and discover a way to keep treading water until they're on the other side of this lull.

We've selected the most practical and thoughtful pieces we've published on career change to help you consider what move you might make, assess whether you're ready to take the leap, and then figure out how to ease into a transition. There's no prescription or formula. Everyone's situation is unique, so we've carefully curated this guide to share the research, insights, and advice from a host of experts to give you the best foundation for navigating your own way.

Career change is a normal part of a long and rich working life. Set aside any nagging self-doubt, and begin the work to turn wishful thinking into a concrete, actionable plan. You can get out of your head and into a new job. Change is within your reach.

—The Editors

SECTION ONE

Understand What's Going On

Wanting to change your career can be exciting—and terrifying. Whether you're coming to this fork in the road because you're ready to branch out in a different direction or because you're stuck in a job that's not a good match, it's easy to think you're the only one who feels this way. That you're in this situation because of choices you made, things you did, missteps you've taken. Things that are unique to you. But the situation you're in isn't just the sum of bad choices or missed opportunities. The need for career change is a normal part of work life; even cyclical.

This section of the guide will help you understand the wider context in which career change happens.

CHAPTER 1

Reawakening Your Passion for Work

by Richard Boyatzis, Annie McKee, and Daniel Goleman

"Am I really living the way I want to live?" We all struggle with the question of personal meaning throughout our lives. The senior executives who read *Harvard Business Review*, for instance, seem to struggle with this question at the high point of their careers. Why? Many executives hit their professional stride in their forties and fifties, just as their parents are reaching the end of their lives—a reminder that all of us are mortal. What's more, many of the personality traits associated with career success, such as a knack for problem solving and sheer tenacity, lead people to stick with a difficult situation in the hope

Adapted from "Reawakening Your Passion for Work" in *Harvard Business Review*, April 2002 (product #R0204G).

of making it better. Then one day, a creeping sensation sets in: Something is wrong. That realization launches a process we have witnessed—literally thousands of times—in our work coaching managers and executives over the past 14 years.

The process is rarely easy, but we've found this type of awakening to be healthy and necessary; leaders need to go through it every few years to replenish their energy, creativity, and commitment—and to rediscover their passion for work and life. Indeed, leaders cannot keep achieving new goals and inspiring the people around them without understanding their own dreams. In this article, we'll look at the different signals that it's time to take stock—whether you have a nagging sense of doubt that builds over time until it's impossible to ignore or you experience a life-changing event that irrevocably alters your perspective. Then we'll describe some strategies for listening to those signals and taking restorative action. Such action can range from a relatively minor adjustment in outlook, to a larger refocusing on what really matters, to practical life changes that take you in an entirely new direction.

When to Say When

When asked, most businesspeople say that passion—to lead, to serve the customer, to support a cause or a product—is what drives them. When that passion fades, they begin to question the meaning of their work. How can you reawaken the passion and reconnect with what's meaningful for you? The first step is acknowledging the signal that it's time to take stock. Let's look at the various feelings that let you know the time has come.

"I feel trapped."

Sometimes, a job that was fulfilling gradually becomes less meaningful, slowly eroding your enthusiasm and spirit until you no longer find much purpose in your work. People often describe this state as feeling trapped. They're restless, yet they can't seem to change—or even articulate what's wrong.

Take the case of Bob McDowell, the corporate director of human resources at a large professional-services firm. After pouring his heart and soul into his work for 25 years, Bob had become terribly demoralized because his innovative programs were cut time and again. As a result, his efforts could do little to improve the workplace over the long term. For years he had quieted his nagging doubts, in part because an occasional success or a rare employee who flourished under his guidance provided deep, if temporary, satisfaction. Moreover, the job carried all the usual trappings of success—title, money, and perks. And, like most people in middle age, McDowell had financial responsibilities that made it risky to trade security for personal fulfillment. Factors such as these conspire to keep people trudging along, hoping things will get better. But clinging to security or trying to be a good corporate citizen can turn out to be a prison of your own making.

"I'm bored."

Many people confuse achieving day-to-day business goals with performing truly satisfying work, so they continue setting and achieving new goals—until it dawns on them that they are bored. People are often truly shaken by this revelation; they feel as if they have just emerged from a spiritual blackout. We saw this in Nick Mimken, the owner of a successful insurance agency, who increasingly felt that something was missing from his life. He joined a book group, hoping that intellectual stimulation would help him regain some enthusiasm, but it wasn't enough. The fact was, he had lost touch with his dreams and was going through the motions at work without experiencing any real satisfaction from the success of his business.

High achievers like Mimken may have trouble accepting that they're bored because it's often the generally positive traits of ambition and determination to succeed that obscure the need for fun. Some people may feel guilty about being restless when it looks like they have it all. Others may admit they aren't having fun but believe that's the price of success. As one manager said, "I work to live. I don't expect to find deep meaning at the office; I get that elsewhere." The problem? Like many, this man works more than 60 hours a week, leaving him little time to enjoy anything else.

"I'm not the person I want to be."

Some people gradually adjust to the letdowns, frustrations, and even boredom of their work until they surrender to a routine that's incompatible with who they are and what they truly want. Consider, for instance, John Lauer, an inspirational leader who took over as president of BFGoodrich and quickly captured the support of top executives with his insight into the company's challenges and opportunities and his contagious passion for the business.

But after he'd been with the company about six years, we watched Lauer give a speech to a class of executive MBA students and saw that he had lost his spark. Over time, Lauer had fallen in step with a corporate culture that was focused on shareholder value in a way that was inconsistent with what he cared about. Not surprisingly, he left the company six months later, breaking from corporate life by joining his wife in her work with Hungarian relief organizations. He later admitted that he knew he wasn't himself by the end of his time at BFGoodrich, although he didn't quite know why.

How did Lauer stray from his core? First, the change was so gradual that he didn't notice that he was being absorbed into a culture that didn't fit him. Second, like many, he did what he felt he "should," going along with the bureaucracy and making minor concession after minor concession rather than following his heart. Finally, he exhibited a trait that is a hallmark of effective leaders: adaptability. At first, adapting to the corporate culture probably made Lauer feel more comfortable. But without strong self-awareness, people risk adapting to such an extent that they no longer recognize themselves.

"I won't compromise my ethics."

The signal to take stock may come to people in the form of a challenge to what they feel is right. Such was the case for Niall FitzGerald, former cochairman of Unilever, when he was asked to take a leadership role in South Africa, which was still operating under apartheid. The offer was widely considered a feather in his cap and a positive sign about his future with Unilever. Until that time, FitzGerald had accepted nearly every assignment, but the South Africa opportunity stopped him in his tracks, posing a direct challenge to his principles. How could he, in good conscience, accept a job in a country whose political and practical environment he found reprehensible?

Or consider the case of a manager we'll call Rob. After working for several supportive and loyal bosses, he found himself reporting to an executive—we'll call him Martin—whose management style was in direct conflict with Rob's values. The man's abusive treatment of subordinates had derailed a number of promising careers, yet he was something of a legend in the company. To Rob's chagrin, the senior executive team admired Martin's performance and, frankly, felt that young managers benefited from a stint under his marine lieutenant–style leadership.

When you recognize that an experience is in conflict with your values, as FitzGerald and Rob did, you can at least make a conscious choice about how to respond. The problem is, people often miss this particular signal because they lose sight of their core values. Sometimes they separate their work from their personal lives to such an extent that they don't bring their values to the office. As a result, they may accept or even engage in behaviors they'd deem unacceptable at home. Other people find that their work *becomes* their life, and business goals take precedence over everything else. Many executives who genuinely value family above all still end up working 12-hour days, missing more and more family dinners as they pursue success at work. In these cases, people may not hear the wake-up call. Even if they do, they may sense that something isn't quite right but be unable to identify it—or do anything to change it.

"I can't ignore the call."

A wake-up call can come in the form of a mission: an irresistible force that compels people to step out, step up, and take on a challenge. It is as if they suddenly recognize what they are meant to do and cannot ignore it any longer.

Such a call is often spiritual, as in the case of the executive who, after examining his values and personal vision, decided to quit his job, become ordained, buy a building, and start a church—all at age 55. But a call can take other forms as well—to become a teacher, to work with disadvantaged children, or to make a difference to the people you encounter every day. Rebecca Yoon, who runs a dry-cleaning business, has come to consider it her mission to connect with her customers on a personal level. Her constant and sincere attention has created remarkable loyalty to her shop, even though the actual service she provides is identical to that delivered by hundreds of other dry cleaners in the city.

"Life is too short!"

Sometimes it takes a trauma, large or small, to jolt people into taking a hard look at their lives. Such an awakening may be the result of a heart attack, the loss of a loved one, or a world tragedy. It can also be the result of something less dramatic, like adjusting to an empty nest or celebrating a significant birthday. Priorities can become crystal clear at times like these, and things that seemed important weeks, days, or even minutes ago no longer matter.

For example, following a grueling and heroic escape from his office at One World Trade Center on September 11, 2001, John Paul DeVito of the May Davis Group stumbled into a church in tears, desperate to call his family. When a police officer tried to calm him down, DeVito responded, "I'm not in shock. I've never been more cognizant in my life." Even as he mourned the deaths of friends and colleagues, he continued to be ecstatic about life, and he's now reframing his priorities, amazed that before this horrific experience he put duty to his job above almost everything else.

DeVito is not alone. Anecdotal evidence suggests that many people felt the need to seek new meaning in their lives after the tragedies of 9/11, which highlighted the fact that life can be cut short at any time. An article in the December 26, 2001, *Wall Street Journal* described two women who made dramatic changes after the attacks. Following a visit to New York shortly after the towers were hit, engineer Betty Roberts quit her job at age 52 to enroll in divinity school. And Chicki Wentworth decided to give up the office and restaurant building she had owned and managed for nearly 30 years in order to work with troubled teens.

But as we've said, people also confront awakening events throughout their lives in much more mundane circumstances. Turning 40, getting married, sending a child to college, undergoing surgery, facing retirement— these are just a handful of the moments in life when we naturally pause, consider where our choices have taken us, and check our accomplishments against our dreams.

Interestingly, it's somehow more socially acceptable to respond to shocking or traumatic events than to any of the others. As a result, people who feel trapped and bored often stick with a job that's making them miserable for far too long, and thus they may be more susceptible to stress-related illnesses. What's more, the quieter signals—a sense of unease that builds over time, for example—can be easy to miss or dismiss because their day-to-day impact is incremental. But such signals are no less important as indicators of the need to reassess than the more visible events. How do you learn to listen to vital signals and respond before it's too late? It takes a conscious, disciplined effort at periodic self-examination.

Strategies for Renewal

There's no one-size-fits-all solution for restoring meaning and passion to your life. However, there are strategies for assessing your life and making corrections if you've gotten off course. Most people pursue not a single strategy but a combination, and some seek outside help while others prefer a more solitary journey. Regardless of which path you choose, you need time for reflection—a chance to consider where you are, where you're going, and where you really want to be. Let's look at five approaches.

Call a time-out

For some people, taking time off is the best way to figure out what they really want to do and to reconnect with their dreams. Academic institutions have long provided time for rejuvenation through sabbaticals—six to 12 months off, often with pay. Some businesses—to be clear, very few—offer sabbaticals as well, letting people take a paid leave to pursue their interests with the guarantee of a job when they return. More often, businesspeople who take time off do so on their own time—a risk, to be sure, but few who have stepped off the track regret the decision.

This is the path Bob McDowell took. McDowell, the HR director we described earlier who felt trapped in his job, stepped down from his position, did not look for another job, and spent about eight months taking stock of his life. He considered his successes and failures and faced up to the sacrifices he had made by dedicating himself so completely to a job that was, in the end, less than fulfilling. Other executives take time off with far less ambitious goals—simply to get their heads out of their work for a while and focus on their personal lives. After a time, they may very happily go back to the work they'd been doing for years, eager to embrace the same challenges with renewed passion.

Still others might want to step off the fast track and give their minds a rest by doing something different. When Nick Mimken, the bored head of an insurance agency, took stock of his life and finally realized he wasn't inspired by his work, he decided to sell his business, keep only a few clients, and take sculpture classes. He then went to work as a day laborer for a landscaper in order to pursue his interest in outdoor sculpture—in particular, stone fountains. Today he and his wife live in Nantucket, Massachusetts, where he no longer works *for* a living but *at* living. He is exploring what speaks to him—be it rock sculpture, bronze casting, protecting wildlife, or teaching people how to handle their money. Nick is deeply passionate about his work and how he is living his life. He calls himself a life explorer.

In any event, whether it's an intense soul-searching exercise or simply a break from corporate life, people almost invariably find time-outs energizing. But stepping out isn't easy. No to-do lists, no meetings or phone calls, no structure—it can be difficult for high achievers to abandon their routines. The loss of financial security makes this move inconceivable for some. And for the many people whose identities are tied up in their professional lives, walking away feels like too great a sacrifice. Indeed, we've seen people jump back onto the train within a week or two without reaping any benefit from the time off, just because they could not stand to be away from work.

Find a program

While a time-out can be little more than a refreshing pause, a leadership or executive development program is a more structured strategy, guiding people as they explore their dreams and open new doors.

Remember John Lauer? Two years after Lauer left BFGoodrich, he was still working with Hungarian refugees (his time-out) and maintained that he wanted nothing to do with running a company. Yet as part of his search for the next phase of his career, he decided to pursue an executive doctorate degree. While in the program, he took a leadership development seminar in which a series of exercises forced him to clarify his values, philosophy, aspirations, and strengths. (See the sidebar "Tools for Reflection" to learn more about some of these exercises.)

In considering the next decade of his life and reflecting on his capabilities, Lauer realized that his resistance to running a company actually represented a fear of replicating his experience at BFGoodrich. In fact, he loved being at the helm of an organization where he could convey his vision and lead the company forward, and he relished working with a team of like-minded executives. Suddenly, he realized that he missed those aspects of the CEO job and that in the right kind of situation—one in which he could apply the ideas he'd developed in his studies—being a CEO could be fun.

With this renewed passion to lead, Lauer returned a few headhunters' calls and within a month was offered the job of chairman and CEO at Oglebay Norton, a $250 million company in the raw-materials business. There he became an exemplar of the democratic leadership style, welcoming employees' input and encouraging his leadership team to do the same. As one of his executives told us, "John raises our spirits, our confidence, and our passion for excellence." Although the company deals in such unglamorous commodities as gravel and sand, Lauer made so many improvements in his first year that Oglebay Norton was featured in *Fortune*, *Business Week*, and the *Wall Street Journal*.

TOOLS FOR REFLECTION

Once you've lost touch with your passion and dreams, the very routine of work and the habits of your mind can make it difficult to reconnect. Here are some tools that can help you break from those routines and allow your dreams to resurface.

Reflecting on the Past

Alone and with trusted friends and advisers, periodically do a reality check. Take an hour or two and draw your "lifeline." Beginning with childhood, plot the high points and the low points: the events that caused you great joy and great sorrow. Note the times you were most proud, most excited, and most strong and clear. Note also the times you felt lost and alone. Point out for yourself the transitions—times when things fundamentally changed for you. Now look at the whole. What are some of the underlying themes? What seems to be ever present, no matter the situation? What values seem to weigh in most often and most heavily when you make changes in your life? Are you generally on a positive track, or have there been lots of ups and downs? Where does luck or fate fit in?

Now switch to the more recent past, and consider these questions: What has or has not changed at work and in life? How am I feeling? How do I see myself these days? Am I living my values? Am I having fun? Do my values still fit with what I need to do at work and with

(*continued*)

TOOLS FOR REFLECTION

what my company is doing? Have my dreams changed? Do I still believe in my vision of my future?

As a way to pull it all together, do a bit of free-form writing. Try finishing the sentence, "In my life I . . . "and "Now I . . ."

Defining Your Principles for Life

Think about the different aspects of your life that are important, such as family, relationships, work, spirituality, and physical health. What are your core values in each of those areas? List five or six principles that guide you in life, and think about whether they are values that you truly live by or simply talk about.

Extending the Horizon

Try writing a page or two about what you would like to do with the rest of your life. Or you might want to number a sheet of paper 1 through 27, and then list all the things you want to do or experience before you die. Don't feel the need to stop at 27, and don't worry about priorities or practicality—just write down whatever comes to you.

This exercise is harder than it seems because it's human nature to think more in terms of what we have to do—by tomorrow, next week, or next month. But with such a short horizon, we can focus only on what's urgent, not on what's important. When we think in terms of the extended horizon, such as what we might do before we die, we open up a new range of possibilities. In our work with leaders who perform this exercise, we've seen a surprising trend: Most people jot down a few career goals, but 80% or more of their lists have nothing to do with work. When they finish the exercise and study their writing, they see patterns that help them begin to crystallize their dreams and aspirations.

Envisioning the Future

Think about where you would be sitting and reading this article if it were 15 years from now and you were living your ideal life. What kinds of people would be around you? How would your environment look and feel? What might you be doing during a typical day or week? Don't worry about the feasibility of creating this life; rather, let the image develop and place yourself in the picture.

Try doing some free-form writing about this vision of yourself, speak your vision into a tape recorder, or talk about it with a trusted friend. Many people report that, when doing this exercise, they experience a release of energy and feel more optimistic than they had even moments earlier. Envisioning an ideal future can be a powerful way to connect with the possibilities for change in our lives.

Another executive we know, Tim Schramko, had a long career managing health care companies. As a diversion, he began teaching part-time. He took on a growing course load while fulfilling his business responsibilities, but he was running himself ragged. It wasn't until he went through a structured process to help him design his ideal future that he realized he had a calling to teach. Once that was clear, he developed a plan for extricating himself from his business obligations over a two-year period and is now a full-time faculty member.

Many educational institutions offer programs that support this type of move. What's more, some companies have developed their own programs because they realize that leaders who have a chance to reconnect with their dreams tend to return with redoubled energy and commitment. The risk, of course, is that after serious reflection, participants will jump ship. But in our experience, most find new meaning and passion in their current positions. In any event, people who do leave weren't in the right job—and they would have realized it sooner or later.

Create "reflective structures"

When leadership guru Warren Bennis interviewed leaders from all walks of life in the early 1990s, he found that they had a common way of staying in touch with what was important to them. They built into their lives what Bennis calls "reflective structures," time and space for self-examination, whether a few hours a week, a day or two a month, or a longer period every year.

For many people, religious practices provide an outlet for reflection, and some people build time into the day or week for prayer or meditation. But reflection does not have to involve organized religion. Exercise is an outlet for many people, and some executives set aside time in their calendars for regular workouts. One CEO of a $2 billion utility company reserves eight hours a week for solitary reflection—an hour a day, perhaps two or three hours on a weekend. During that time, he might go for a long walk, work in his home shop, or take a ride on his Harley. However you spend the time, the idea is to get away from the demands of your job and be with your own thoughts.

Increasingly, we've seen people seek opportunities for collective reflection as well, so that they can share their dreams and frustrations with their peers. On his third time heading a major division of the Hay Group, Murray Dalziel decided to build some reflection into his life by joining a CEO group that meets once a month. In a sense, the group legitimizes time spent thinking, talking, and learning from one another. Members have created a trusting community where they can share honest feedback—a scarce resource for most executives. And all gain tangible benefits, as people exchange tips on how to fix broken processes or navigate sticky situations.

Work with a coach

Our own biases and experiences sometimes make it impossible for us to find a way out of a difficult or confusing situation; we need an outside perspective. Help can come informally from family, friends, and colleagues, or it can come from a professional coach skilled at helping people see their strengths and identify new ways to use them. We won't discuss more traditional therapy in this article, but it is, of course, another alternative.

When Bob McDowell, the HR director, stepped out of his career, he sought out a variety of personal and professional connections to help him decide how to approach the future. Working with an executive coach, McDowell was able to identify what was important to him in life and translate that to what he found essential in a job. He could then draw clear lines around the aspects of his personal life he would no longer compromise, including health and exercise, time with his family, personal hobbies, and other interests. In the end, he found his way to a new career as a partner in an executive search business—a job he'd never considered but one that matched his passion for helping people and the companies they work for. What's more, his soul-searching had so sparked his creativity that in his new position he combined traditional organizational consulting with the search process to discover unusual possibilities. Instead of a typical executive search, he helps companies find employees who will bring magic to the business and to the relationships essential to success.

What did the coach bring to McDowell's self-reflection? Perhaps the chief benefit was a trusting, confidential relationship that gave him the space to dream—something executives shy away from, largely because the expectations of society and their families weigh on them so heavily. Like many, McDowell began this process assuming that he would simply narrow his priorities, clarify his work goals, and chart a new professional path. But to his surprise, his coach's perspective helped him see new opportunities in every part of his life, not just in his work.

Sometimes, however, a coach does little more than help you recognize what you already know at some level. Richard Whiteley, the cofounder of a successful international consulting firm and author of several business best-sellers, felt that he wasn't having as much fun as he used to; he was restless and wanted a change. To that end, he began to do some work on the side, helping businesspeople improve their effectiveness through spiritual development. He was considering leaving his consulting practice behind altogether and concentrating on the spiritual work—but he was torn. He turned to a spiritual leader, who told him, "Forget the spiritual work and concentrate on the work you've been doing." Only when forced to choose the wrong path could Richard recognize what he truly wanted to do. Within a few months, Richard had devoted himself to writing and speaking almost exclusively on spirituality and passion in work—and he's thriving.

Find new meaning in familiar territory

It's not always feasible to change your job or move somewhere new, even if your situation is undesirable. And frankly, many people don't want to make such major changes. But it is often easier than you might think to make small adjustments so that your work more directly reflects your beliefs and values—as long as you know what you need and have the courage to take some risks.

Back to Niall FitzGerald, who was confronted with the decision over whether to live and work in South Africa. A strong and principled person as well as a good corporate citizen, FitzGerald eventually decided to break with company culture by accepting the job on one unprecedented condition: If over the first six months or so he found his involvement with the country intolerable, he would be allowed to take another job at Unilever, no questions asked. He then set forth to find ways to exert a positive influence on his new work environment wherever possible.

As the leader of a prominent business, FitzGerald had some clout, of course, but he knew that he could not take on the government directly. His response: Figure out what he *could* change, do it, and then deal with the system. For example, when he was building a new plant, the architect showed FitzGerald plans with eight bathrooms—four each for men and women, segregated by the four primary racial groups, as mandated by law. Together, the eight bathrooms would consume one-quarter of an entire floor.

FitzGerald rejected the plans, announcing that he would build two bathrooms, one for men and one for women, to the highest possible standards. Once the plant was built, government officials inspected the building, noticed the discrepancy, and asked him what he planned to do about it. He responded, "They're not segregated because we chose not to do so. We don't agree with segregation. These are very fine toilets . . . you could have your lunch on the floor . . . . I don't have a problem at all. You have a problem, and you have to decide what you are going to do. I'm doing nothing." The government did not respond immediately, but later the law was quietly changed. FitzGerald's act of rebellion was small, but it was consistent with his values and was the only stand he could have taken in good conscience. Living one's values in this way, in the face of opposition, is energizing. Bringing about change that can make a difference to the people around us gives meaning to our work, and for many people, it leads to a renewed commitment to their jobs.

For Rob, the manager who found himself reporting to an abusive boss, the first step was to look inward and admit that every day would be a challenge. By becoming very clear about his own core values, he could decide moment to moment how to deal with Martin's demands. He could determine whether a particular emotional reaction was a visceral response to a man he didn't respect or a reaction to a bad idea that he would need to confront. He could choose whether to do what he thought was right or to collude with what felt wrong. His clarity allowed him to stay calm and focused, do his job well, and take care of the business and the people around him. In the end, Rob came out of a difficult situation knowing he had kept his integrity without compromising his career, and in that time, he even learned and grew professionally. He still uses the barometer he developed during his years with Martin to check actions and decisions against his values, even though his circumstances have changed.

Another executive we've worked with, Bart Morrison, ran a nonprofit organization for 10 years and was widely considered a success by donors, program recipients, and policy makers alike. Yet he felt restless and wondered if a turn as a company executive—which would mean higher compensation—would satisfy his urge for a new challenge. Morrison didn't really need more money, although it would have been a plus, and he had a deep sense of social mission and commitment to his work. He also acknowledged that working in the private sector would not realistically offer him any meaningful new challenges. In our work together, he brainstormed about different avenues he could take while continuing in the nonprofit field, and it occurred to him that he could write books and give speeches. These new activities gave him the excitement he had been looking for and allowed him to stay true to his calling.

It's worth noting that executives often feel threatened when employees start asking, "Am I doing what I want to do with my life?" The risk is very real that the answer will be no, and companies can lose great contributors. The impulse, then, may be to try to suppress such exploration. Many executives also avoid listening to their own signals, fearing that a close look at their dreams and aspirations will reveal severe disappointments, that to be true to themselves they will have to leave their jobs and sacrifice everything they have worked so hard to achieve.

But although people no longer expect leaders to have all the answers, they do expect their leaders to be open to the questions—to try to keep their own passion alive and to support employees through the same process. After all, sooner or later most people will feel an urgent need to take stock—and if they are given the chance to heed the call, they will most likely emerge stronger, wiser, and more determined than ever.

Richard Boyatzis is Distinguished University Professor, professor in departments of organizational behavior, psychology, and cognitive science at Case Western Reserve University, and adjunct professor at ESADE. His MOOCs have over 720,000 participants enrolled from over 215 countries. He has authored more than 200 articles and eight books, including *Becoming a Resonant Leader: Develop Your Emotional Intelligence, Renew Your Relationships, Sustain Your Effectiveness* (Harvard Business Review Press, 2008) with coauthors Annie McKee and Frances Johnston. **Annie McKee** is a senior fellow at the University of Pennsylvania Graduate School of Education where she teaches and leads the PennCLO Executive Doctoral Program and the MedEd Master's program. Her latest book is *How to Be Happy at Work: The Power of Purpose, Hope, and Friendship* (Harvard Business Review Press, 2017). **Daniel Goleman** is codirector of the Consortium for Research on Emotional Intelligence in Organizations at Rutgers University. His latest book is *Altered Traits: Science Reveals How Meditation Changes Your Mind, Brain, and Body* (Avery, 2017) with coauthor Richard J. Davidson. Boyatzis, McKee, and Goleman are coauthors of *Primal Leadership: Unleashing the Power of Emotional Intelligence* (Harvard Business Review Press, 2013).

CHAPTER 2

Why So Many of Us Experience a Midlife Crisis

by Hannes Schwandt

A midcareer crisis can happen to anyone. Canadian psychoanalyst and organizational consultant Elliott Jaques coined the term *midlife crisis*: that period in our lives when we come face-to-face with our limitations, our restricted possibilities, and our mortality. This experience hits even those who objectively have the most fulfilling jobs. When it does, the crisis inflicts pain on the individual suffering it and causes productivity losses for employers. Yet, the phenomenon remains stigmatized and underresearched, leaving crucial questions unanswered.

Adapted from content posted on hbr.org, April 20, 2015 (product #H020PC).

What are the causes? Why does this malaise seem to strike in midlife? And how can those who are stuck in its grips shake themselves loose?

What Causes the Crisis?

An emerging literature in economics has started to investigate what's happening during midlife, providing insights that might help people and firms better handle these painful and costly episodes. Analyzing a nationwide survey from the United Kingdom, a group of economists working with professor Andrew Oswald of The University of Warwick found that the job satisfaction of the average employee deteriorates dramatically in midlife. Midcareer crises are, in fact, a widespread regularity rather than the misfortune of a few individuals. But here's the good news: In the second half of people's working lives, job satisfaction increases again, in many cases reaching even higher levels than earlier in their career—essentially forming a U-shaped curve.

Subsequent research discovered that this age-related U-shape in job satisfaction is part of a much broader phenomenon. A similar midlife nadir is detectable in measures of people's overall life satisfaction and has been found in more than 50 countries. On average, life satisfaction is high when people are young, then starts to decline in their early thirties, bottoming out between the midforties and midfifties before increasing again to levels as high as during young adulthood. And this U-curve occurs across the entire socioeconomic spectrum, hitting senior-level executives as well as blue-collar workers and stay-at-home parents. It affects childless couples as well as single people or parents of four. In short, a midcareer crisis does not discriminate.

So what's driving the midlife nadir in job and life satisfaction if it's independent of people's life circumstances? And if it's such a widespread phenomenon, why does it seem to catch us by surprise? To answer these questions, I analyzed a unique longitudinal German survey that followed 23,000 individuals from 1991 to 2004 in which people reported their current life satisfaction as well as the satisfaction they expect to have in five years. Since the same individuals are interviewed each year, it's possible to see if people accurately predicted their future life satisfaction.

Young people, it turns out, are overly optimistic, expecting significant increases in life satisfaction rather than anticipating the slide down the U-curve. Young adults typically believe that they'll "beat the average": that they'll be the lucky ones who end up with a top job, a happy marriage, and healthy children. Neuroscientists believe that overoptimism is based on biased information processing in the brain, which makes it difficult to correct overly rosy expectations in the young (this bias might actually be evolutionarily efficient, as a powerful driver for seeking progress).

As we age, things often don't turn out as nicely as we had planned. We may not climb up the career ladder as quickly as we wished. Or we do, only to find that prestige and a high income are not as satisfying as we expected them to be. At the same time, high expectations about the future adjust downward. Midlife essentially becomes a time of double misery, made up of disappointments and evaporating aspirations. Paradoxically, those who objectively have the least reason to complain (say, if they have a desirable job) often suffer the most. They feel ungrateful and disappointed with themselves particularly because their discontent seems so unjustified—which creates a potentially vicious circle. The *Atlantic*'s contributing editor Jonathan Rauch described several such cases (including his own) in his cover story on midlife crisis, "The Real Roots of Midlife Crisis," for which he interviewed me about my research.

It's at the bottom of the U-curve (the midfifties, according to the German data) when expected life satisfaction aligns with current satisfaction levels. People come to terms with how their life is playing out. At the same time, the aging brain learns to feel less regret about missed chances, as brain studies have shown. This combination of accepting life and feeling less regret about the past is what makes life satisfaction increase again. And since people over 50 tend to *underestimate* their future satisfaction, these increases come as an unexpected pleasant surprise, which further raises satisfaction levels.

As a whole, these findings tell a story in which the age U-shape in job (and overall life) satisfaction is driven by unmet aspirations that are painfully felt in midlife but beneficially abandoned and felt with less regret during old age. Importantly, in the German study, I found this pattern regardless of people's socioeconomic status, their gender, or whether they lived in East or West Germany, despite the cultural differences in the decade right after unification. Periods of "midcareer crisis" seem to be part of a natural developmental process, driven by biology rather than the specifics of a particular job. Hence, drastic career changes are unlikely to make you better off. If the burned-out Wall Street lawyer and the dissatisfied NGO activist were to change seats, perhaps neither would end up more content.

How to Cope with a Midcareer Crisis

The data seems to suggest that if you're in the throes of a midcareer crisis, maybe you should just wait it out until the U-curve's upward slope is reached. But there is more we can do in the face of midcareer malaise:

- **At the individual level,** acknowledging midcareer dissatisfaction as a normal and temporary stage in your work life provides a light at the end of the tunnel when you feel like there's no hope. Moreover, hearing that it's OK to feel regret from unmet aspirations helps you break the vicious circle of disappointment about feeling discontent.

- **At the firm level,** HR could create midcareer mentoring programs. Mentoring is usually directed at early career stages and continues only informally through the rest of the career. My findings suggest that those in a midcareer low can learn from their older colleagues who have already gone through the valley and emerged feeling less regret, having adapted to life's circumstances. A corporate culture that openly addresses midcareer discontent could support employees in this reorientation process, helping them explore new opportunities—within the firm.

While a midcareer crisis can be a painful time in life, it can also be an opportunity to reflect and to reevaluate personal strengths and weaknesses. Whether you choose to wait out the discontent or make a drastic change in hopes of a brighter tomorrow, rest assured that this too shall pass. Take heart if you find yourself in the depths of this U-shaped curve, because things can only look up from here.

———————

Hannes Schwandt is an assistant professor in the economics department of the University of Zurich and the Jacobs Center for Productive Youth Development. Connect with him at https://hschwandt.com/.

What Do You Think You Want to Do?

If you don't know what you want to do—only that what you're currently doing isn't it—this part of the book is for you, as it will help you think through what your next career move could be. We often think of our dream jobs, but even considering (in detail) what the job of our nightmares looks like is useful information to gather and reflect on. This section of the guide offers questions and exercises to help you explore and flesh out potential new identities.

CHAPTER 3

Developing a Strategy for a Life of Meaningful Labor

by Brian Fetherstonhaugh

In a world of constant disruption, both opportunity and uncertainty exist in the workplace. All of us need a new way of thinking about work and taking personal responsibility for our careers, which last 45 years and beyond.

Over the past three decades, I have been counseling and mentoring people and conducting research on the topic of career strategy. I've been struck by how many people at all stages of life are extremely anxious about

Adapted from content posted on hbr.org, September 5, 2016 (product #H0341F).

their career but have invested little time in creating a strategy for it. If you are one of those people, take the time to change that: Set aside a day to create a plan for pursuing the most purposeful and rewarding work possible. Whether you're a millennial, a Gen Xer, or a baby boomer, here are five actions you can take to get your career strategy rolling.

Calculate How Much Longer You'll Be Working

Most people vastly underestimate how long a career lasts, so do some simple math. Tally up how many years, days, and hours you expect to be working, even part-time. Hint: The current average retirement age in the United States is 65, but it's going up. Many are choosing—or needing—to work well into their seventies.

Figure Out What Career Stage You Are At

There are three major career stages, each lasting about 15 years. You'll need to adjust as you pass through them.

- **Stage one: start of career through midthirties.** Make this your time to discover, learn, and try different things. Sign up for some special assignments at work. Take an online course. Volunteer for a not-for-profit organization that might stretch your skills. Be open to opportunities inside and outside of your company if you believe they can accelerate your learning. You're sure to take a few wrong turns, but even mistakes and learning what you don't like are valuable.

- **Stage two: late thirties to early fifties.** This is your time to reach high by building on strengths and differentiating yourself from others. You'll want to find your sweet spot, which is the intersection of what you love, what you're good at, and what the world values. (The chapters in this section of the book will help you discover and define that intersection.)

- **Stage three: midfifties and beyond.** At age 50, you could easily have more than 20 years of work life left. Your work should be sustainable and keep a reasonable pace that could last for decades. One of your main areas of focus at this stage should be to stay fresh. Nobody wants to hire someone who is only concerned with the past. Stay relevant and well connected so that you can become a practitioner of "active wisdom" for years to come. Try some reverse mentoring—share some of your expertise with a younger colleague in exchange for what they know about today. Remain a lifelong learner. Read up on current technologies and emerging industries and think about how the principles and knowledge you have accumulated could be applied into the future.

Take Inventory of How Much "Career Fuel" You Have

The people who are most successful in the long term are those who have an abundant supply of what I call "career fuel": transportable skills, meaningful experiences, and enduring relationships.

Transportable skills include problem solving, being adept at persuading others, getting things done, and knowing how to take smart risks. These are skills you can carry with you from job to job, company to company, and industry to industry.

Meaningful experiences take us out of our comfort zone and make us more adaptable to changes in our job environment. Think travel, intense community service, launching products, or starting your own business.

Enduring relationships are perhaps the most powerful form of career fuel: the connections, experts, critical colleagues, and mentors who make a huge difference in your career progression.

Assess whether your fuel levels are growing, stagnating, or perhaps even declining. Ask yourself what you can do in the next year to replenish them. You don't always need to change jobs or industries to add fuel. Look for new pathways within your own organization through a special assignment, job rotation, expanded responsibilities, or structured training.

Grade Your Current Work Situation

Don't depend on your gut or how you feel late on a Friday evening to evaluate your job satisfaction. Get objective by asking these four questions: Are you learning? Are you having impact? Are you having fun? And, finally, are you being fairly rewarded?

Regarding the last one: Look at the full package of rewards, including salary, benefits, vacation, and workplace flexibility. Is it fair for what you are contributing to the organization? How does it compare to the going rate in the marketplace?

What do the answers to these questions show you? Could you boost some of the low ratings? Can they be fixed in your current situation, or should you look elsewhere?

Invest Your Time Wisely

Time is the currency of our lives, and how we spend it speaks volumes about what we think is important. Sketch a simple pie chart of how you have spent your time over the past couple of months, using categories such as work, family, community, health, and relaxation.

What does your pie chart say about how you're investing in yourself? What balance of work and play is sustainable for the journey ahead? Are you devoting enough time to the things that really make you happy, even in small doses? Should you adjust your time as you transition from one stage to another? Are you using your precious time to build fuel? How does your time portfolio relate to your answers to the job satisfaction questions?

A career is a long ride, and it's more than just work: It's a huge part of life. Take time to think strategically about your career journey. Only one person will be with you for the whole ride, and that's you. Don't just worry about it—take some action.

———————

Brian Fetherstonhaugh is global chief talent officer of The Ogilvy Group and the author of *The Long View: Career Strategies to Start Strong, Reach High, and Go Far* (Diversion Publishing, 2016).

CHAPTER 4

Turn the Job You Have into the Job You Want

by Amy Wrzesniewski, Justin M. Berg, and Jane E. Dutton

A 30-year-old midlevel manager—let's call her Fatima— is struggling at work, but you wouldn't know it from outward appearances. A star member of her team in the marketing division of a large multinational foods company, Fatima consistently hits her benchmarks and goals. She invests long hours and has built relationships with colleagues that she deeply values. And her senior managers think of her as one of the company's high potentials.

Reprinted from *Harvard Business Review*, June 2010 (product #R1006K).

But outside the office, Fatima (who asked not to be identified by her real name) would admit that she feels stagnant in her job, trapped by the tension between day-to-day demands and what she really wants to be doing: exploring how the company can use social media in its marketing efforts. Twitter, her cause-marketing blog, and mobile gadgets are her main passions. She'd like to look for another job, but given the slow recovery from the recession, sticking it out seems like her best (and perhaps only) option. "I'm still working hard," she tells a friend. "But I'm stuck. Every week, I feel less and less motivated. I'm beginning to wonder why I wanted this position in the first place."

Sound familiar? Over the past several years, we've spoken with hundreds of people, in a variety of industries and occupations, who, like Fatima, are feeling stuck—that dreaded word again. According to a recent survey of 5,000 U.S. households by The Conference Board, only 45% of those polled say they are satisfied with their jobs—down from about 60% in 1987, the first year the survey was conducted.

If you're in this situation, and changing roles or companies is unrealistic given the tough economy, what can you do? A growing body of research suggests that an exercise we call "job crafting" can be a powerful tool for re-energizing and reimagining your work life. It involves redefining your job to incorporate your motives, strengths, and passions. The exercise prompts you to visualize the job, map its elements, and reorganize them to better suit you. In this way, you can put personal touches on how you see and do your job, and you'll gain a greater sense of control at work—which is especially critical at a time when you're probably working longer and harder and expecting to retire later. Perhaps job crafting's best feature is that it's driven by you, not your supervisor.

This exercise involves assessing and then altering one or more of the following core aspects of work:

- **Tasks.** You can change the boundaries of your job by taking on more or fewer tasks, expanding or diminishing their scope, or changing how they are performed. A sales manager, for instance, might take on additional event planning because he likes the challenge of organizing people and logistics.

- **Relationships.** You can change the nature or extent of your interactions with other people. A managing director, for example, might create mentoring relationships with young associates as a way to connect with and teach those who represent the future of the firm.

- **Perceptions.** You can change how you think about the purpose of certain aspects of your job, or you can reframe the job as a whole. The director of a nonprofit institution, for instance, might choose to think of his job as two separate parts: one not particularly enjoyable (the pursuit of contributions and grants) and one very meaningful (creating opportunities for emerging artists). Or the leader of an R&D unit might come to see her work as a way of advancing the science in her field rather than simply managing projects.

Our research with a range of organizations—from *Fortune* 500 companies to small nonprofits—indicates that employees (at all levels, in all kinds of occupations) who try job crafting often end up more engaged and satisfied with their work lives, achieve higher levels of performance in their organizations, and report greater personal resilience.

For their part, organizations have a lot to gain by enabling job crafting. Most job-redesign models put the onus on managers to help employees find satisfaction in their work; in reality, leaders rarely have sufficient time to devote to this process. Job crafting lets managers turn the reins over to employees, empowering them to become "job entrepreneurs." And when pay resources are constrained or promotions impossible, job crafting may give companies a different way to motivate and retain their most-talented employees. It can even help transform poor performers.

Despite these benefits, however, job crafting can be easy to overlook: Time pressures and other constraints may compel you to see your job as a fixed list of duties. Or you may be afraid of getting mired in office politics and stepping on other people's toes simply because you're unhappy at work. Job crafting requires—and ultimately engenders—a different mindset, however: Your job comprises a set of building blocks that you can reconfigure to create more engaging and fulfilling experiences at work.

Diagramming Your Job

Back at the multinational foods company, Fatima is still frustrated. What would happen if she engaged in job crafting? She's already been reflecting on her dissatisfaction, albeit in no systematic way. Job crafting would give her the means to diagram a more ideal—but still realistic—version of her job, one better aligned with her motives, strengths, and passions.

First, she looks at the present makeup of her job. In her "before" diagram, Fatima uses a series of squares to represent the tasks that her job comprises, with larger squares representing time-intensive tasks and increasingly smaller squares representing tasks to which she devotes less time. (See figure 4-1.)

She notices that she's spending lots of time monitoring her team's performance, answering questions, and

FIGURE 4-1

Fatima's "before" diagram

Once she has created her before diagram, this midlevel marketing manager immediately sees that she's spending lots of time on tasks that don't engage her passions—for instance, monitoring her team's performance, answering questions, and directing market research— and much less on tasks that are meaningful to her.

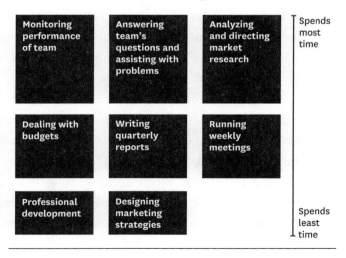

directing market research. She's spending a fair number of hours setting budgets, writing reports, and running meetings. And she's spending very little time on critical tasks such as professional development and designing marketing strategies. These tasks are in the smallest squares. Looking at the full sweep of her job in this way gives Fatima a clear sense—truly at a glance—of exactly where she is devoting her time and energy.

Next, she concentrates on changes that would increase her engagement at work. This "after" diagram will serve as the visual plan for her future. (See figure 4-2.)

She begins by identifying her motives, strengths, and passions—three important considerations in determining which aspects of her job will keep her engaged and inspire higher performance. Each will be represented by a different shade of gray. Her main motives, for instance, are cultivating meaningful relationships and achieving personal growth. She plugs these into light gray ovals. Fatima takes stock of her core strengths: one-on-one communication and technical savvy. These appear in medium gray ovals. And she highlights her passions: teaching others and using and learning new technology—in dark gray ovals.

Then, using her "before" diagram as a frame of reference, Fatima creates a new set of task blocks whose size represents a better allocation of her time, energy, and attention. To take advantage of how well "designing marketing strategies" suits her motives, strengths, and passions, she not only moves it from a small to a medium block but also adds "that use social media" to this newly expanded task. To incorporate even more social media

FIGURE 4-2

Fatima's "after" diagram

In Fatima's after diagram, it's easier to see how she can connect her tasks to her motives, strengths, and passions. For instance, one of her motives is to cultivate meaningful relationships and achieve personal growth. Her strengths include her one-on-one communication skills and technical savvy. And among her passions are teaching others and using and learning about new technology.

In this after diagram, the sizes of the blocks represent a better allocation of Fatima's time, energy, and attention. The borders around groups of tasks suggest the common purpose they serve. By rearranging the shapes on the page, Fatima gains a greater appreciation for how the different elements of her job come together.

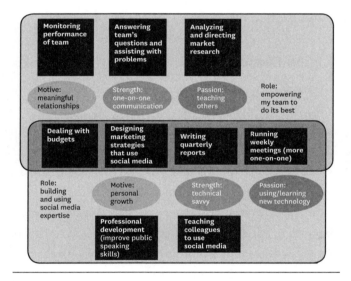

into her job, she adds a small task block to represent "teaching colleagues to use social media." And for those tasks that do not fit her as well, she makes a note to adapt them (for instance, using "professional development" to "improve public speaking skills").

She draws rectangles around groups of tasks that she thinks serve a common purpose or role. For example, she identifies "building and using social media expertise" as one role. Framing her roles in this way is meaningful to her because it taps in to her key strengths and passions. By rearranging the shapes, Fatima gains a greater appreciation for how the elements of her job come together.

A New Outlook

Fatima then moves to the final step of the exercise, in which she considers the challenges she will probably face in making her new job configuration a reality. She would like to use her technical savvy to help other marketing teams and departments take advantage of social media, but she is concerned about encroaching on their work or insulting them by offering her expertise. With her "after" diagram in hand, Fatima takes another look at the list of projects sitting in her inbox and begins to consider how to incorporate social media into them.

- **Tasks.** Fatima identifies two possibilities: a new snack food aimed at teens and a cross-company initiative to improve communication between Marketing and Sales. Fatima thinks a campaign involving Facebook and Twitter could help build buzz around the snack food—and reveal to the organization the benefits and limitations of reaching out to a new demographic. And by launching a blog, Fatima and her colleagues in Marketing could track initiatives and communications from members of the Sales division.

- **Relationships.** Fatima recognizes, of course, that she'll need support to establish the technological presence she envisions for these two projects. She must build or refocus her ties to others in the company in order to learn about the best ways to move forward. She recalls that Steve Porter is constantly fiddling with the latest gadgets in weekly interdepartmental meetings and that he is known for the clever ways he uses social media to keep salespeople in the loop. She decides to approach him for help. Within a month, Steve's and her own employees' support has unleashed a wave of interest in and knowledge about how to put technology closer to the heart of the division's work. Her initiatives have become testing grounds for using social media to accomplish other important goals. Fatima has been recognized as the driver of these programs and finds that managers from other divisions are coming to her to learn more about how they might use her ideas in their own projects—all of which is encouraging her to be bolder in introducing new ideas and technology.

- **Perceptions.** Rather than thinking of her work as a daily slog, Fatima begins to see herself as an innovator at the intersection of marketing and technology. And she views herself as an entrepreneurial pioneer who is unafraid of experiments that could bridge those worlds. She also, to her pleasure, recognizes that rather than taking her away from her prescribed goals, her passion for deploying technology in pursuit of these objectives gives her a more fulfilling way to approach them.

Ivan's Story

In another company, in another part of the world, Ivan Carter is caught between a rock and a hard place. But the source of angst for this 45-year-old operations manager at a global office products company is quite different from Fatima's. He's a solid B player with a dedicated and successful team. Ivan leads a group that serves Latin America, and he reports to both the head of global operations and the head of the Latin America group. His relationship with the latter is great, but the operations head is often nonresponsive or even hostile when Ivan needs information or support. All his efforts to strengthen the relationship have been met with silence. He likes his job, but he often leaves the office with his stomach in knots.

Ivan knows he can either accept the reality of his toxic relationship with the head of operations or change his situation. So, during his next phone meeting with the head of Latin America, he pushes a bit to explore what interests her most about the role of the operations group in that region. She sees the group as becoming more critical for cost savings as economic recovery drags on—a major focus for the CEO, as well. Ivan spots an opportunity. He can build on what is already a good relationship by directing more of his efforts to special projects that will save money in that region. Sensing a chance to craft his job, Ivan focuses more and more of his time and energy on this aspect of his work, which wins him exposure and credit as the projects he takes on create significant savings for the company. As a bonus, he spends more time interacting with the Latin America head while meeting his responsibilities to the operations head without having to interact with him as much. After several months, Ivan learns that the Latin America head has highly recommended him to others in the C-suite.

Fatima focused first on tasks and then on relationships. By centering his job crafting primarily on relationships (the ones that energized rather than depleted him), Ivan was able to figure out how to change his job for the better.

The Limits of Job Crafting

Not all job crafting is beneficial. It can be stressful if as a result you take on too much or alter tasks without understanding your manager's goals. Since job crafting is something you can do on your own, it's important to be open about the process. Your manager may even be able to help you identify opportunities for redistributing tasks in complementary ways. After all, one person's dreaded assignment may be another's favorite.

To win others' support for your job crafting, do these three things:

- Focus on deploying an individual or organizational strength that will create value for others. For instance, Fatima positioned her work to enhance what other teams were doing, while Ivan found a way to help meet the objectives of the Latin America group.

- Build trust with others (typically your supervisor). Fatima assured her supervisor that she wouldn't let tasks slide and that some of her newer tasks could become central to the organization. Ivan was careful to align his efforts with his role, building trust with the head of the Latin America group.

- Direct your job-crafting efforts toward the people who are most likely to accommodate you. Fatima reached out to Steve Porter because he was interested in her plans to bring technology into the heart of her job tasks. Ivan realized that his time would be wasted pursuing a toxic relationship and instead focused on a more promising one.

Job crafting is a simple visual framework that can help you make meaningful and lasting changes in your job—in good economies and bad. But it all has to start with taking a step back from the daily grind and realizing that you actually have the ability to reconfigure the elements of your work.

The bottom line? Make sure that you are shaping your job—not letting your job shape you.

Amy Wrzesniewski is an associate professor of organizational behavior at the Yale School of Management. **Justin M. Berg** is an assistant professor of organizational behavior at the Stanford Graduate School of Business. **Jane E. Dutton** is the Robert L. Kahn Distinguished University Professor of Business Administration and Psychology at the University of Michigan's Ross School of Business. She is cofounder of the Center for Positive Organizations at Ross.

CHAPTER 5

Two Ways to Clarify Your Professional Passions

by Robert Steven Kaplan

Have you ever noticed that highly effective people almost always say they love what they do? If you ask them about their good career fortune, they will likely advise that you have to love what you do in order to perform at a high level of effectiveness. They will talk about the critical importance of having a long-term perspective and real passion in pursuing a career. Numerous studies of highly

---

Adapted from content posted on hbr.org, March 30, 2015 (product #H01YUI).

effective people point to a strong correlation between believing in the mission, enjoying the job, and performing at a high level.

So why is it that people are often skeptical of the notion that passion and career should be integrally linked? Why do people often struggle to discern their passions and then connect those passions to a viable career path? When people hear the testimony of a seemingly happy and fulfilled person, they often say, "That's easy for them to say *now*. They've made it. It's not so easy to follow this advice when you're sitting where I'm sitting!" What they don't fully realize is that connecting their passions to their work was a big part of how these people eventually made it.

Passion is about excitement. It has more to do with your heart than your head. It's critical because reaching your full potential requires a combination of your heart *and* your head. In my experience, your intellectual capability and skills will take you only so far.

Regardless of your talent, you will have rough days, months, and years. You may get stuck with a lousy boss. You may get discouraged and feel like giving up. What pulls you through these difficult periods? The answer is *your passion*: It is the essential rocket fuel that helps you overcome difficulties and work through dark times. Passion emanates from a belief in a cause or the enjoyment you feel from performing certain tasks. It helps you hang in there so that you can improve your skills, overcome adversity, and find meaning in your work and in your life.

In talking to more-experienced people, I often have to get them to mentally set aside their financial obligations, their role in the community, and the expectations of friends, family, and loved ones. It can be particularly difficult for midcareer professionals to understand their passions because, in many cases, the cost of changing jobs or careers feels so huge to them that it's not even worth considering. As a result, they try not to think too deeply about whether they like what they're doing.

The problem for many midcareer people is that they're experiencing a plateau that is beginning to alarm them and diminish their career prospects. This plateau is often a by-product of lack of passion for the job. It may be that the nature of the job has changed or the world has changed, and the mission and tasks of their career no longer arouse their passions. In other cases, nothing has changed except the people themselves. They simply want more meaning from their lives and professional careers.

Of course, these questions are never fully resolved. Why? It's because there are many variables in play, and we can't control all of them. The challenge is to be self-aware.

That's difficult, because most of our professional days are chaotic. In fact, life is chaotic, and, sadly, we can't usually predict the future. It feels as if there's no time to reflect. So how are you supposed to get perspective on these questions?

I suggest that you try several exercises. These exercises will help you increase your self-awareness and develop your ability to better understand your passions. They also encourage you to pay closer attention to and be more aware of the tasks and subjects you truly find interesting and enjoyable.

Your Best Self

This exercise involves thinking back to a time when you were at your best. You were great! You did a superb job, and you really enjoyed it. You loved what you were doing while you were doing it, and you received substantial positive reinforcement.

Remember the situation. Write down the details. What were you doing? What tasks were you performing? What were the key elements of the environment, the mission, and the nature of the impact you were making? Did you have a boss, or were you self-directed? Sketch out the complete picture. What did you love about it? What were the factors that made it enjoyable and helped you shine?

If you're like most people, it may take you some time to recall such a situation. It's not that you haven't had these experiences; rather, you have gotten out of the habit of thinking about a time when you were at your best and enjoying what you were doing.

After sketching out the situation, think about what you can learn from this recollection. What are your insights regarding the nature of your enjoyment, the critical environmental factors, the types of tasks you took pleasure in performing, and so on? What does this recollection tell you about what you might enjoy now? Write down your thoughts.

Mental Models

Another approach to helping you think about your desires and passions is to use mental models. That is, assume *xyz*, and then tell me what you would do—and why. Here are examples of these models:

- If you had one year left to live, how would you spend it? What does that tell you about what you enjoy and what you have a passion for?

- If you had enough money to do whatever you wanted, what job or career would you pursue?

- If you knew you were going to be highly successful in your career, what job would you pursue today?

- What would you like to tell your children and grandchildren about what you accomplished in your career? How will you explain to them what career you chose?

- If you were a third party giving advice to yourself, what would you suggest regarding a career choice?

Although these mental models may seem a bit silly or whimsical, I urge you to take the time to try them, consider your answers, and write them down. You're likely to be surprised by what you learn. Each of them attempts to help you let go of fears, insecurities, and worries about the opinions of others—and focus on what you truly believe and desire.

Passion is critical in reaching your potential. Getting in touch with your passions may require you to give your fears and insecurities a rest and focus more on your hopes and dreams. You don't need to immediately decide what action to take or assess whether your dream is realistic. There is an element of brainstorming in this effort: You don't want to kill ideas before you've considered them. Allow yourself to focus on the *what* before you worry about the *how*. These exercises are about self-awareness, first and foremost. It is uncanny how much more likely you are to recognize opportunities if you're aware of what you're looking for.

Robert Steven Kaplan is president and chief executive of the Federal Reserve Bank of Dallas. Previously, he was the senior associate dean for external relations and Martin Marshall Professor of Management Practice in Business Administration at Harvard Business School. He is the author of three books: *What You Really Need to Lead* (Harvard Business Review Press, 2015), *What You're Really Meant to Do* (Harvard Business Review Press, 2013, from which this article is adapted), and *What to Ask the Person in the Mirror* (Harvard Business Review Press, 2011).

CHAPTER 6

For Career Direction, Use Your Imagination

by Bill Barnett

Do you know what you want to do with your career? What if you don't? You first must imagine what the right career field might be. That's easy to say, but hard to do. There are productive ways to look for clues about what might work for you.

Tommy (whose name has been changed) shifted career direction after doing imagination exercises. He had a full-time job and was pursuing an MBA on nights and weekends. If he stayed with his employer after graduating, he would not only move onto a management track,

Adapted from content posted on hbr.org, June 28, 2012.

but the company would also refund his tuition cost. He had assumed he would take full advantage of this deal, but when he went through what he called the "dream job exercise," he realized that his current position was wrong for him (read on to discover how to imagine your own dream job). He wasn't excited about where he worked, and he didn't want to move into management there.

Through his dream job exercise, Tommy was able to consider fields that emphasized intellectual exploration. He'd felt some of that curiosity the first year or two in his current job, but that had faded. He recalled that he'd once been interested in pursuing a PhD and becoming a professor. That's ultimately what he decided to do.

If you need ideas about your future direction, create your own dream job exercise. Follow these three steps:

1. **Imagine extreme jobs.** Spend 10 minutes describing the perfect position—one that fully fills your needs and is plausible for you. Think of a vivid, concrete example (like becoming an electronics product manager or starting a restaurant). Describe the job's characteristics: what you'd do each day, how the organization would work, your impact, and so on. Be expansive. Do it again for one or two other "perfect" jobs.

   Then, imagine the opposite—a job you'd feel was horrible, even though others might disagree. Go through the same process you used to describe your dream jobs. Be expansive, and repeat the process for two other jobs you think you'd hate.

2. **Consider extreme strengths.** Look to your own capabilities for inspiration. Take your top strength, and imagine a few fields where it would be the right fit. What might be possible? For this moment at least, the sky's the limit. Take a second strength and go through the same process. Do it a third time.

3. **Recall past interests.** Think back to your time in high school, college, or your first job. What did you enjoy most? How did you spend your time off? Look back to pivotal career decisions, how and why you made them, and how they turned out. These are personal case studies. Why did you make those decisions? How important are those criteria now?

As you develop new skills and knowledge in school and at work, you may discard things along the way. That's natural and is often a sign of maturity. But you may also be leaving talents behind that belong in your future.

These three steps bring to mind what you care most about in your work. Take a look at your lists and see where they align with different fields of work. Once you have a promising idea, research that field and talk to people who know it. Find out what it's like and if it matches your interests.

Once you've found something that sounds right to you, ensure you're the right fit. Consider the unique skills you'd bring to the job you'd like to have. If you're not equipped for that position but you're determined to make it happen, figure out how to upgrade your qualifications to create that opportunity, whether it's starting with a lower position in the field, going back to school, or developing skills using online resources.

Keep in mind that this is an early exercise, fit for those who don't know where to start or who may want to change careers. The answer isn't black and white. You're looking for ideas to consider, not absolute proof. With a little effort and imagination, following these steps will give you good ideas for fields to explore.

———————

Bill Barnett led the strategy practice at McKinsey & Company and has taught career strategy to graduate students at Yale University and Rice University. He now applies business strategy concepts to careers. He is the author of *The Strategic Career: Let Business Principles Guide You* (Stanford Business Books, 2015).

Is Career Change Right for You?

Do you have the necessary skills to transfer to a new field? Can you afford a pay cut? Could you relocate your family? This section of the guide will help you articulate the risks you're facing so that you can begin to mitigate them.

CHAPTER 7

Not Taking Risks Is the Riskiest Career Move of All

by Anne Kreamer

Mark was a survivor. Until he was fired in 2012, six months shy of his fiftieth birthday, he'd done everything right: He'd risen through the ranks of the book publishing industry, from editorial assistant to associate editor to senior editor, then gone into management as an editor in chief. But as ebooks and Amazon destabilized the industry and waves of consolidation contracted available jobs, Mark (whose name has been changed) admits today that he hadn't "paid attention to the writing on the wall." He confesses that he'd spent the 18 months prior

---

Adapted from content posted on hbr.org, April 16, 2015 (product #H020L9).

to being fired living in denial as his team was reorganized. "Despite that," he says, "I clung to my job rather than starting to think about how to leave. At that point, I couldn't conceive of a life outside the confines of corporate publishing, of not being at the center of the club I'd been a part of—and a star in—since the age of 21."

Mark's story is a cautionary tale for us all. In my experience, Mark's kind of wishful thinking—that things will sort themselves out on their own—rarely works out. *Not* taking action has costs that can be as consequential as taking risks; it's simply less natural to calculate and pay attention to the "what-ifs" of inaction. In today's marketplace, where jobs and job categories are being invented and becoming obsolete at an accelerating rate, I'd argue that the riskiest move one can make is to assume that their industry or job is secure. Just ask former employees of Countrywide, British Petroleum, or *Newsweek* if you doubt me.

Research I conducted in 2012, 2013, and 2014 with the global advertising agency J. Walter Thompson for my book *Risk/Reward: Why Intelligent Leaps and Daring Choices Are the Best Career Moves You Can Make* suggests that anxiety about our job futures weighs on us heavily these days. More than half of the respondents to our surveys, from people all over the United States, in a wide range of ages, in positions ranging from janitors to CEOs, were thinking of changing not just their jobs but their *careers*. Think about that. Half of all Americans long to do something dramatically different with their working lives from what they are currently doing.

But it's hard to jettison a career that's been decades in the making in the pursuit of something new. There's an enormous gap between dreaming about doing something different, particularly if one has spent years building skills and rising through the ranks, and actually making a change. It's terrifying to think about not using one's hard-earned law degree and letting go of years invested in the law firm partner track in order to write for television, as an acquaintance of mine has done. Most people dream but fail to act.

What stops us? There are all sorts of complicated financial and behavioral barriers to risk-taking—loss and risk aversion, the sunk-cost fallacy, poor planning—but basically it boils down to the fact that as human beings, we are wired to resist giving up the known for the unknown. None of us tolerates ambiguity well, particularly when the losses and gains underpin our livelihoods or the projected long-term happiness of our families. Psychologically, particularly during tough economic times, people feel compelled to hold on to an unsatisfactory job rather than gamble on something with uncertain odds, even if it might be better in the long run. And we all have different levels of innate risk tolerance that inform our calculus for evaluating probable gains and losses. How can we turn self-defeating inaction into sensible action? Two ways to mitigate the risk of trying on a new career are to build a robust network and to break a big, hairy problem into small, actionable steps.

Build Vibrant Networks

In *Working Identity: Unconventional Strategies for Reinventing Your Career*, Herminia Ibarra, an organizational behavior professor at London Business School, writes that people's existing "contacts [don't] help them reinvent themselves . . . the networks we rely on in a stable job are rarely the ones that lead us to something new and different." Stanford sociologist Mark Granovetter discovered that the contacts most helpful to people looking for new jobs were neither their closest friends nor new acquaintances but rather people with whom they had relatively *weak* ties that had been forged and maintained over several years. In addition, the more different their contacts' occupations were from their own jobs, the more likely people were to successfully make a major career change. There's a reason, when we're interested in making a 45- or 90-degree career shift, why most jobs suggested by headhunters tend not to feel right. The majority of people we know in one line of work can only imagine us continuing to do the same thing. Meeting more people who are employed in a wide range of professions strengthens our ability to imagine ourselves doing something different. That makes a career change feel more achievable and less risky.

Take Small Steps Toward Big Goals

Perhaps the biggest impediment to change in our working lives is the sense that any significant change has to be all or nothing. *I either quit my miserable job or just suck it up and grind along. I've got to make a compre-*

hensive business plan before I test whether my English muffin/croissant hybrid and baked-goods truck can generate enough income for me to live. I'm good at structuring logical arguments so I should quit sales and become a lawyer. Big challenges feel too risky to navigate, so we stay put. Instead, we need to break problems into small actions. A more moderate approach to considering a shift to a law career would be to test-drive the profession by becoming a paralegal before assuming the expensive three-year commitment of getting a law degree. The amateur cook with a killer recipe could approach a local bakery with his novel product to see if they'd be willing to sell it. This would result in getting market feedback before crafting a business plan for a new venture. The person in the miserable job could volunteer weekends at an organization they think might make them happier. This would help them learn what the work is really like from the inside before chucking it all on a dream that may be a fantasy. Armed with real-world data, each of those hypothetical career changers would have more clarity about what to do next. The trick is to start with the immediately, manageably doable and *do*.

We need to continue to find new challenges and set goals—and then acquire the skills to meet those challenges and achieve those goals. Committing to goals also provides structure and meaning to our lives that leads to more overall happiness, says Sonja Lyubomirsky, a psychologist at the University of California, Riverside. She quotes the writer G. K. Chesterton in this regard: "There is one thing which gives radiance to everything. It is the idea of something around the corner."

Real life, by necessity, is improvisational and inter-active, crafted incrementally through our responses to the particular circumstances at this moment in time, and the next, and then the next. As author Tom Peters wrote, "I have said and mean with all my heart I've only learned one thing 'for sure' in 48 years: WTTMSW. Whoever tries the most stuff wins."

Anne Kreamer is the former executive vice president and worldwide creative director for Nickelodeon and Nick at Nite. Her books include *Risk/Reward: Why Intelligent Leaps and Daring Choices Are the Best Career Moves You Can Make* (Random House, 2015), *It's Always Personal: Navigating Emotion in the New Workplace* (Random House, 2013), and *Going Gray: What I Learned About Beauty, Sex, Work, Motherhood, Authenticity, and Everything Else That Really Matters* (Little, Brown and Company, 2007).

CHAPTER 8

Can You Actually Afford to Change Your Career?

by Russell Clayton

Who wouldn't want a meaningful career and better balance between work and home? For many of us, it's finances that keep us from making a career change. Sure, our current job has lost its spark, but it's stable. Dependable. Reliable. Steady. We worry and wonder: *What would a career change do to our bank accounts? To our way of life? To our family?* We assume that a major reinvention would involve a gap between paychecks when we'd leave our job and break into a new field. Sometimes we think (or we know) that the career we'd love would fill our days with more meaning but pay us less (significantly less, even).

Take Steve. A well-respected HR manager in the public sector, leading his own recruitment team and earning a decent salary. Or Amanda, an elementary school teacher in the inner city with 11 years under her belt. Or Brandon, a rising star at a large, well-known nonprofit organization. Those who know these three individuals would likely have characterized their careers as successful. But Steve, Amanda, and Brandon all left those jobs and made a midcareer transition.

What drove them to abandon established careers, steady incomes, and security? For Steve, it was a desire to find meaningful work. Although he was doing well and liked his team and his company, he felt that his workdays alternated between feeling every minute tick by and putting out fires. While the pay was good, he felt like his role didn't have a deeper purpose. His heart wasn't in it.

Amanda found the instructional part of her job as an inner-city teacher extremely fulfilling, but she was discouraged by paperwork and trying to "teach to the test." She noted, "I was only teaching 30% of the time, and the rest I was filling out forms." Gradually her frustration with these aspects of her job mounted, and she became burned-out.

Brandon took the leap and left his stable nonprofit job to seek a better work-life balance. He wasn't intending to change his career until a conversation with his young daughter revealed that she felt as though he worked too much and spent too little time with her. While he was making significant improvements to his organization's way of doing business, the 80-hour weeks were wrecking his home life. He had to make a change.

Like Steve, Amanda, and Brandon, we're all drawn to career change for different reasons. But for many of us, worry about the potential financial risk in such a change turns into a roadblock we never surmount. While every situation is different, here are some factors to consider that may help reduce your financial concerns and make a radical move feel more achievable.

Try Living on Your New Income

If you're worried that your new job will pay less, test out your estimated salary. Take what you anticipate earning, and live on that for two to four months. Better yet, live on *less* than you anticipate earning. This will give you a realistic picture of what life would look like, from an income perspective, in your new career. For starters, review your budget to see where your current income is going. If you don't already have a budget, take a look at the past six months of your credit card bills and checkbook and debit card logs to see where you've been spending. Once you have a budget in place, go over your expenses—both fixed and discretionary—to see where you could trim. How much should you cut back? That depends on the anticipated size of your income reduction. If your new career would pay you 90% of what you make in your current gig, then you can probably manage the transition by reducing what you spend on groceries, canceling your cable TV service, or foregoing meals out. If your new career will result in a sizable pay cut, you'll need to be more aggressive. Look at your major spending categories to identify cost-saving opportunities. Are there more-affordable housing options in your area? Can you cut your commuting costs by using public transportation? While you may be reluctant to take such drastic steps for an experiment, use this period to explore alternatives and assess the impact of making changes. Say you want to downsize your home to reduce your monthly payment. How feasible is it to find cheaper housing in your area? If the real estate market where you live is down, it could be difficult to get out of your current home.

When Amanda planned to quit her teaching job, she knew the move to working part-time at a nonprofit would come with an approximate $30,000 reduction in her salary based on an exploratory meeting she'd had with the organization's leader. Amanda was pregnant but planned to go back to work part-time immediately following her daughter's birth. However, complications during her pregnancy forced her to take an extended period of strict bed rest. Her teaching benefits didn't cover short-term disability. She could not work; she did not earn an income. "This accidental trial run was rough, and we had to watch every penny . . . but it showed us that we *could* make it on less money," she reported. Though Amanda didn't choose the timing or duration of her trial run, you can map out an intentional reduced budget for a set period of time to get a realistic picture of what life might be like if you earn less.

At the end of your trial, revisit your budget or your banking statements to see how you did. What was the resulting impact on what you have saved—and what you owe? How did it feel? Are you willing to make those cutbacks more permanent? Take this opportunity to scrutinize your spending to see if there are additional expenses, like Netflix and Amazon Prime memberships, that could be eliminated.

Create an Emergency Fund

What if something unexpected happens in your new career? Or what if you can't sell your home? Building or adding to an existing emergency fund will help ease the stress and worry of beginning a new career. A good rule of thumb is to have three to six months' worth of living expenses saved up. While this advice is somewhat standard among financial advisers, aim for the higher end of that spectrum to give you some breathing room, just in case your transition doesn't go as planned. The more financial cushion you have, the more time you can take to find another job if it comes to that.

So how can you build an emergency fund? For starters, you could earmark your income tax return or yearly bonus. As you try out your new salary, take the dollars per month you've cut from your expenses as part of your experiment and add it to your emergency fund. Or extend your trial run and choose to live frugally for a longer period so you can stash away more cash. Steve and his wife chose that option to save money before he returned to graduate school. In addition to the usual cost-saving measures, they sold one of their cars and shared one car between them. This not only got rid of a monthly car payment, it also cut down on what they spent on gas, insurance, and maintenance. Your adventure into frugal living might look like Steve's, or you might cut costs elsewhere. If you're driving a vehicle with a high monthly payment, can you trade it in for something cheaper?

Can you limit discretionary expenses (coffee, subscriptions, memberships)? Can you think outside the box and consider far-reaching ways you could save money? Maybe you could adopt a minimalist wardrobe, with a few essential, interchangeable, easy-care pieces. Doing so would allow you to reduce your clothing allowance and curb your dry-cleaning bills.

Of course, living frugally requires a lot of motivation. It sounds dreadful. It can feel dreadful. Focusing on *why* you're making these cuts can help. You're scrimping to have the career you desire instead of a job that simply pays the bills. Tap your support system for ideas to save—and to cope. And be sure to reward yourself once in a while. Celebrate your successes. For every $1,000 saved toward your emergency fund, treat yourself to something nice (but reasonable), like a dinner out.

Assess Your Household's Risk Tolerance

How do you feel about risk? How does your spouse feel about it? Everyone's tolerance for risk is different. Take Brandon. He considers himself risk averse, so when he made the move from nonprofit leadership to starting his own business, he did so with caution. He built up his emergency cushion by pulling his child out of day care and keeping her at home with him. Once he'd launched his business, he continued to mitigate risk by being extremely selective in which clients he'd take on. To provide a level of job security and predictable income, Brandon only contracted with organizations that would agree to let him manage their conferences for two or more years.

Likewise, Margaret, a single mother of two who is admittedly risk averse, didn't transition from tenure-track college instructor to HR consultant until she found a job with the salary she needed. Had the money not been right, she would not have made the move. She knew her budget and her risk tolerance; she did not have a partner's salary or health insurance to fall back on. She wasn't willing to compromise or to put her family in a bad spot just to make the change.

Assessing how comfortable you are with risk will help you see which choices are good for you—and which ones you should leave on the table. Quantify your level of risk tolerance by taking one of the many self-assessments you can find online, such as the financial risk tolerance questionnaire developed by Virginia Tech's Ruth Lytton and University of Georgia's John Grable. If your risk tolerance is fairly low but your proposed career change is one that will reduce your income by 75%, then you'll probably want to rethink your choice. On the other hand, if a questionnaire suggests you have a high tolerance for risk, a drastic reduction in salary may not be a deterrent for you.

Create a Backup Plan

Knowing how you feel about risk will also give you a sense of how solid your backup plan should be. If you're highly cautious about change, reduce your stress by fleshing out a Plan B (and C and D, if necessary). Take all of the reflecting and imagining you did to get to where you are to consider what you might do if your new gig doesn't work out as you'd hoped. Steve, Amanda, and

Brandon all had working spouses whose income provided a safety net during their career transitions. Beyond that, all three noted that their extended families had offered financial assistance if necessary. Beyond money, Steve, Amanda, and Brandon maintained their relationships with colleagues in their prior workplaces and industries. Knowing that they existed and could be tapped into in the event that they needed to return to their old field provided some reassurance.

In addition to maintaining ties with former colleagues in your network, stay abreast of what's happening in your old industry. If you're leaving the mortgage loan field, keep up with regulations and policies that govern that area. Or if you're leaving an industry that requires a certification (such as a CPA), maintain any licenses or credentials until you're well entrenched into your new career. You'll mitigate your stress and risk during the transition and give yourself a greater opportunity to return to your former industry should you need to.

Manage Expectations

Check in with your family members to discuss the implication of your change on their lives. These conversations should focus on schedule adjustments, income variances, and spending habits that will make the transition a success. Setting expectations for what your new life will look like—especially financially—will leave room for few surprises and less resulting disappointment once income levels change. Amanda, Brandon, and Steve all had multiple conversations with their spouses over time before they switched careers. Amanda and her husband were accustomed to dining out a few times per week while she was employed as a teacher. So they talked about discretionary spending they'd eliminate—meals out—in order to live on the reduced income her career transition would entail. When she changed jobs and dining out became a rare treat instead of a regular occurrence, it took getting used to, but no one was caught off guard.

Steve's career change required different stages of setting and managing expectations with his wife, as his transition came in two phases that took place over four years. First he moved from HR manager to college instructor, which came with a $15,000-per-year reduction in income. After holding that job for a year and a half, he returned to graduate school full-time—going without a steady income for three years. Steve and his wife deliberated for a full year before he moved into the unpaid student phase of his career change. "While we did roll the dice financially, we arrived at that point mutually," Steve notes. "We knew what we were getting into." To assess their situation, Steve and his wife looked into apartment rental prices and cost-of-living data for the various cities where he applied to graduate school. They also looked at employment data in those cities to assess his wife's chances of finding a job if they were to move there. All this research and discussion paid off, as they discovered they were willing and able to live frugally in a handful of the cities where he applied to graduate school.

The financial implications of a career change weigh heavily on the mind of anyone considering doing something different. You'll have to do some deep thinking, conduct some tough conversations, and make some lifestyle changes. But moving to a career that makes you happy to get up and go to work every day will help you remember that your short-term sacrifices are in service of your long-term goals. Your transition won't happen overnight or come without bumps in the road, but don't lose hope. It can be done.

Russell Clayton is a faculty member at the University of South Florida and the author of *In Search of Work-Life Balance* (Blue Moon Books, 2016). Connect with him at www.russellclayton.net.

CHAPTER 9

How to Stay Stuck in the Wrong Career

by Herminia Ibarra

Everyone knows a story about a smart and talented businessperson who has lost his or her passion for work, who no longer looks forward to going to the office yet remains stuck without a visible way out. Most everyone knows a story, too, about a person who ditched a 20-year career to pursue something completely different—the lawyer who gave it all up to become a writer or the auditor who quit her accounting firm to start her own toy company—and is the happier for it.

Reprinted from *Harvard Business Review*, December 2002 (product #R0212B).

"Am I doing what is right for me, or should I change direction?" is one of the most pressing questions in the midcareer professional's mind today. The numbers of people making major career changes, not to mention those just thinking about it, have risen significantly over the last decade and continue to grow. But the difference between the person who yearns for change yet stays put and the person who takes the leap to find renewed fulfillment at midcareer is not what you might expect. Consider the following examples.

Susan Fontaine made a clean break with her unfulfilling past as partner and head of the strategy practice at a top consulting firm. But the former management consultant—her name, like the names of the other people I studied, has been changed for this article—had not yet had the time to figure out a future direction. When a close client offered her the top strategy job at a *Financial Times* 100 firm, she took it. She was ready for change, and the opportunity was too good to pass up. To her dismay, the position—though perfect according to what she calls "the relentless logic of a post-MBA CV"—was no different from her old job in all the aspects she had been seeking to change. Two weeks into the new role, she realized she had made a terrible mistake.

After a four-week executive education program at a top business school, Harris Roberts, a regulatory affairs director at a major health care firm, was ready for change. He wanted bottom-line responsibility, and he itched to put into practice some of the cutting-edge ideas he had learned in the program. His longtime mentor, the company's CEO, had promised, "When you come back, we'll give you a business unit." But upon Harris's return, a complicated new product introduction delayed the long-awaited-for transition. He was needed in his old role, so he was asked to postpone his dream. As always, Harris put the company first. But he was disappointed; there was no challenge anymore. Resigned to waiting it out, he created for himself a "network of mentors," senior members of the firm whom he enlisted to guide his development and help him try to land the coveted general management role. Eighteen months later, he was still doing essentially the same job.

A milestone birthday, upheaval in his personal life, and a negative performance evaluation—the first of his career—combined to make a "snapping point" for Gary McCarthy. After business school, the former investment banker and consultant had taken a job at a blue-chip firm by default, biding his time until he found his "true passion." Now, he decided, it was time to make a proactive career choice. Determined to get it right, Gary did all the correct things. He started with a career psychologist who gave him a battery of tests to help him figure out his work interests and values. He talked to headhunters, friends, and family and read best-selling books on career change. By his own account, none of the advice was very useful. He researched possible industries and companies. He made two lists: completely different professions involving things he was passionate about and variations on what he was already doing. A year later, a viable alternative had yet to materialize.

When I consider the experiences of these people and dozens of others I have studied over the past few years, there can be no doubt: Despite the rhetoric, a true change of direction is very hard to swing. This isn't because managers or professionals are typically unwilling to change. On the contrary, many make serious attempts to reinvent themselves, devoting large amounts of time and energy to the process at great professional and personal risk. But despite heroic efforts, they remain stuck in the wrong careers, not living up to their potential and sacrificing professional fulfillment.

Many academics and career counselors observe this inertia and conclude that the problem lies in basic human motives: We fear change, lack readiness, are unwilling to make sacrifices, sabotage ourselves. My in-depth research (see the sidebar "Studying Career Change" for an explanation of my methods) leads me to a different conclusion: People most often fail because they go about it all wrong. Indeed, the conventional wisdom on how to change careers is in fact a prescription for how to stay put. The problem lies in our methods, not our motives.

In my study, I saw many people try a conventional approach and then languish for months, if not years. But by taking a different tack, one I came to call the practice of working identity, they eventually found their way to brand-new careers. The phrase "working identity," of course, carries two meanings. It is, first, our sense of self in our professional roles, what we convey about ourselves to others and, ultimately, how we live our working lives. But it can also denote action—a process of applying effort to reshape that identity. Working our identity, I found, is a matter of skill, not personality, and therefore can be learned by almost anyone seeking professional

STUDYING CAREER CHANGE

Certain career transitions have been thoroughly studied and are well understood: a move into a position of greater managerial responsibility and organizational status, a transfer to a similar job in a new company or industry, a lateral move into a different work function within a familiar field. But few researchers have investigated how managers and professionals go about making a true change of direction.

My research is an in-depth study of 39 people who changed, or were in the process of trying to change, careers. Determining the magnitude of any work transition is highly subjective. Who, apart from the person who has lived through it, can say whether a shift is radical or incremental? After interviewing dozens of people who were making very different kinds of career moves, I settled on a three-part definition of career change.

Some of the people in my study made significant changes in the context in which they worked, most typically jumping from large, established companies to small, entrepreneurial organizations or to self-employment or between the for-profit and nonprofit sectors. Others made major changes in the content of the work, sometimes leaving occupations, such as medicine, law, or academia, that they had trained for extensively. The majority made significant changes in both what they did and where they did it, but most important, all experienced a feeling of having reached

(continued)

STUDYING CAREER CHANGE

a crossroad, one that would require psychological change.

My sample ranged in age from 32 to 51, with an average of 41. I chose this range not to coincide with the infamous midlife crisis but to study a group of people with enough experience in one career to make a shift to another high-stakes endeavor. Sixty-five percent of the participants were men. Almost half of the subjects lived and worked outside the United States, mostly in France and the United Kingdom. It was a highly credentialed sample: All had college degrees, and about three-fourths held graduate or professional degrees (business, science, law, and so on). They represented all walks of managerial and professional life, including business management, law, finance, academia, medicine, science, and technology.

Some of the interviews were retrospective, with people who had already completed their changes. With people at earlier stages of the transition, I conducted an average of three interviews over two to three years. The interviews were open-ended, typically beginning with: "Tell me about your career to date." Between the interviews, I had email exchanges and telephone conversations with participants to keep track of their progress. I supplemented this core study with many shorter interviews involving a range of career change professionals, including headhunters, venture capitalists, career counselors, and outplacement specialists.

renewal. But first we have to be willing to abandon every-thing we have ever been taught about making sound ca-reer decisions.

A Three-Point Plan

We like to think that the key to a successful career change is knowing what we want to do next, then using that knowledge to guide our actions. But studying people in the throes of the career change process (as opposed to afterward, when hindsight is always 20/20) led me to a startling conclusion: Change actually happens the other way around. Doing comes first, knowing second.

Why? Because changing careers means redefining our working identity. Career change follows a first-act-and-then-think sequence because who we are and what we do are tightly connected, the result of years of action; to change that connection, we must also resort to action—exactly what the conventional wisdom cautions us against.

Conventional career change methods—Susan's "logi-cal" CV progression, Harris's networking, and Gary's planning—are all part of what I call the "plan and imple-ment" model of change. It goes like this: First, determine with as much clarity and certainty as possible what you really want to do. Next, use that knowledge to identify jobs or fields in which your passions can be coupled with your skills and experience. Seek advice from the people who know you best and from professionals in tune with the market. Then simply implement the resulting action steps. Change is seen as a one-shot deal: The plan-and-implement approach cautions us against making a move before we know exactly where we are going.

It all sounds reasonable, and it is a reassuring way to proceed. Yet my research suggests that proceeding this way will lead to the most disastrous of results, which is to say no result. So if your deepest desire is to remain indefinitely in a career that grates on your nerves or stifles your self-expression, simply adhere to that conventional wisdom, presented below as a foolproof, three-point plan.

Know Thyself

Like Gary McCarthy, most of us are taught to begin a career change with a quest for self-knowledge. Knowing, in theory, comes from self-reflection, in solitary introspection or with the help of standardized questionnaires and certified professionals. Learning whether we are introverted or extroverted, whether we prefer to work in a structured and methodical environment or in chaos, whether we place greater value on impact or income helps us avoid jobs that will again prove unsatisfying. Having reached an understanding of his or her temperament, needs, competencies, core values, and priorities, a person can go out and find a job or organization that matches.

Gary did all these things. Armed with his test results, he researched promising companies and industries and networked with a lot of people to get leads and referrals. He made two lists of possibilities: "conformist" and "nonconformist." But what happened from there, and what consumed 90% of the year he spent looking for a new career, is what the conventional models leave out: a lot of trial and error.

Gary started with several rounds of talking with traditional companies and headhunters. Next, he tried to turn a passion or a hobby into a career: He and his wife wrote a business plan for a wine-tour business. The financials were not great, so they dropped it. Next, Gary pursued his true fantasy career: He got certified as a scuba instructor and looked into the purchase of a dive operation. He soon learned, though, that his dream job was unlikely to hold his interest over the long term (and thus was not worth the economic sacrifice). So he went back to the headhunters and traditional companies, only to reconfirm that he did not want what they had to offer. Next, he identified entrepreneurs he admired and looked for ways to get his foot in their doors. He explored freelancing, trying to get short-term projects in exciting young companies. But a precise match did not materialize.

Certainly the common practice of looking back over our careers and identifying what we liked and disliked, what we found satisfying and not satisfying, can be a useful tool. But too often this practice is rooted in the profound misconception that it is possible to discover one's "true self," when the reality is that none of us has such an essence. (See the sidebar "Our Many Possible Selves" for a discussion of why one's true self is so elusive.) Intense introspection also poses the danger that a potential career changer will get stuck in the realm of daydreams. Either the fantasy never finds a match in a real-world, paycheck-producing job or, unlike Gary, we remain emotionally attached to a fantasy career that we do not realize we have outgrown.

OUR MANY POSSIBLE SELVES

What is identity? Most traditional definitions—the ones that form the foundation for most career advice—are based on the notion of an "inner core" or a "true self." By early adulthood, these theories suggest, a person has formed a relatively stable personality structure, defined by his or her aptitudes, preferences, and values. Excavating this true self—often forgotten in a dead-end pursuit of fame, fortune, or social approval—should be the starting point of any career reorientation, according to conventional wisdom. With the appropriate self-knowledge, obtained via introspection and psychological testing, a person can more easily search for the right "match" and avoid the mistakes of the past. This true-self definition corresponds perfectly to the plan-and-implement method: Once we find the self, all that remains is execution.

The work of Stanford cognitive psychologist Hazel Markus and other behavioral scientists, however, offers a different definition of identity, one that is more consistent with what I have discovered: We are many selves. And while these selves are defined partly by our histories, they are defined just as powerfully by our present circumstances and our hopes and fears for the future.

Our possible selves—the images and fantasies we all have about who we hope to become, think we should become, or even fear becoming—are at the heart of the career change process. Although conventional wisdom says pain—a self we fear becoming—is the only driver for change, in reality pain can create paralysis. We change only when we have enticing alternatives that we can feel, touch, and taste. That is why working identity, as a practice, is necessarily a process of experimenting, testing, and learning about our possible selves.

Take Gary McCarthy, the former investment banker and consultant profiled in the main article. The set of possible selves he considered is typical in its number and range. It included a "ditch it all and open a tour-guide business in the south of France with my wife" self; a socially respectable "junior partner" self that his parents would have endorsed; a youthful, outdoorsy, "follow your passion" self who renounced convention and wanted to open a scuba business; a "responsible spouse and future parent" self who wanted to make good dual-career decisions; a "corporate drone at age 50, full of regrets" self; an "apprentice" self who learned at the elbow of an admired entrepreneur; and a practical, reasonable, "go to a traditional company where I can combine my backgrounds in banking and consulting" self.

Conventional wisdom would say that the scope of his list of possibilities was evidence that he lacked focus and wasn't ready for change. But within the

(continued)

OUR MANY POSSIBLE SELVES

working identity framework, it was precisely this variety that allowed him to find a truly good fit. Certain possible selves are concrete and tangible, defined by the things we do and the company we keep today; others remain vague and fuzzy, existing only in the realm of private dreams, hypothetical possibilities, and abstract ideas. By bringing the possibilities—both desired and feared, present and future—more sharply into focus, we give ourselves a concrete base of experience from which to choose among them.

We learn who we have become—in practice, not in theory—by testing fantasy and reality, not by "looking inside." Knowing oneself is crucial, but it is usually the outcome of—and not a first input to—the reinvention process. Worse, starting out by trying to identify one's true self often causes paralysis. While we wait for the flash of blinding insight, opportunities pass us by. To launch ourselves anew, we need to get out of our heads. We need to *act*.

Consult Trusted Advisers

If you accept the conventional wisdom that career change begins with self-knowledge and proceeds through an objective scrutiny of the available choices, who should you turn to for guidance? Conventional wisdom has it that you should look to those who know you best and those who know the market. Friends and family—with whom you share a long history—can offer insight into your true nature, and they have your best interests at heart; professionals add a dose of pragmatism, keeping you grounded in the realities of the marketplace.

In times of change and uncertainty, we naturally take comfort in our enduring connections with friends and family. But when it comes to reinventing ourselves, the people who know us best are the ones most likely to hinder rather than help us. They may wish to be supportive, but they tend to reinforce—or even desperately try to preserve—the old identities we are trying to shed. Early in his career, Gary discovered that his close circle would not be much help. "I wanted to do something different but was shocked to realize that people were already pigeonholing me," he says. "I tried to brainstorm with friends and family about what other things I might do. All the ideas that came back were a version of 'Well, you could get a middle management job in a finance department of a company.' Or 'You could become a trainee in a management program.'" John Alexander, an investment banker hoping to make a go of fiction writing, reports that he had often discussed his career predicament with his friends and family. "They would tend to say, 'I can see why writing might be interesting, but you've got a very good job, and do you really want to jeopardize that?'"

Mentors and close coworkers, though well meaning, can also unwittingly hold us back. Take Harris Roberts, the health care company director who wanted to assume a general management role. The people around him, who were invested in his staying put, only mirrored his normal doubts about moving outside his comfort zone. His mentors cared about him and held the power to make his desired change a reality. But they made a fence, not a gateway, blocking the moves that would lead to career change. By talking only to people who inhabited his immediate professional world, people whose ideas for him didn't go beyond the four walls, Harris seriously limited himself. Not only did he lack outside market information, but these coworkers could no more let go of their outdated image of a junior Harris than he himself could.

Headhunters and outplacers, today's career change professionals, can keep us tethered to the past just as effectively. We assume, rightly, that they have the market perspective we lack—but we forget that they are in the business of facilitating incremental moves along an established trajectory. At midcareer, however, many people are no longer looking to "leverage past experience in a different setting." They want to invent their own jobs and escape the shackles of corporate convention, in some cases to do something completely different. What Susan Fontaine, the management consultant, experienced is typical: "I found headhunters unhelpful, basically. I would say, 'Here are my skills; what else might I do?' And they kept saying, 'Why don't you move to Andersen?' or, 'Why don't you try Bain?' All they could suggest was exactly the same thing. I kept saying, 'I'm quite clear I don't want to do that, and if I did want to do that, I would not come to you. I can do that on my own.'"

So if self-assessment, the advice of close ones, and the counsel of change professionals won't do it, then where can we find support for our reinvention? To make a true break with the past, we need to see ourselves in a new light. We need guides who have been there and can understand where we are going. Reaching outside our normal circles to new people, networks, and professional communities is the best way to both break frame and get psychological sustenance.

Think Big

We like to think that we can leap directly from a desire for change to a single decision that will complete our reinvention—the conventional wisdom would say you shouldn't fool yourself with small, superficial adjustments. But trying to tackle the big changes too quickly can be counterproductive. Just as starting the transition by looking for one's true self can cause paralysis rather than progress, trying to make one big move once and for all can prevent real change.

When Susan Fontaine decided to leave her consulting career, it was with good reason. A single mother of two, she was finding the travel and other demands on her personal life increasingly intolerable. She quit her job and resolved to spend some time exploring her options. That resolve vanished, however, when financial pressure coincided with a flattering offer to join the management team of a former client. She accepted the new position only to discover that its demands would be very similar to those of the position she had left. "I thought, 'What have I done?'" she later told me. "I had had the opportunity to leave all that!" By hoping to solve all her problems in one fell swoop, Susan made a change that amounted to no change at all. Two weeks into the new job, she resigned.

As much as we might want to avoid endless procrastination, premature closure is not the answer. It takes time to discover what we truly want to change and to identify the deeply grooved habits and assumptions that are holding us back. The lesson of Susan's story is that trying to make a single bold move can bring us back to square one all too quickly. A longer, less linear transition process may leave us feeling that we are wasting time. But as we will see below, taking smaller steps can allow a richer, more grounded redefinition of our working identity to emerge.

Three Success Stories

Although they floundered, victims of conventional wisdom, Gary McCarthy, Harris Roberts, and Susan Fontaine eventually moved on to a different—and more successful—approach. Gary is now at a media company he admires, working as an internal venture capitalist, a role that allows him to use his skill set in consulting and finance but grants him great creative latitude and total ownership of his results. Harris is president and COO of a growing medical device company and very much involved in setting the strategic direction of his new firm. Susan is working with nonprofits, bringing her strategy expertise to this sector and loving her work.

None of them followed a straight and narrow route. Gary dabbled in wine tours and flirted with buying a scuba diving operation before settling on what his wife called a more normal path. Harris had his prized general management role snatched from under him a second time as the result of a corporate restructuring. He considered leaving for a biotech startup but realized that he simply did not have the appetite for such a risky move. Susan set up temporarily as a freelance consultant, landing traditional consulting projects to pay the bills and using her discretionary time to explore a more varied portfolio of assignments.

Their experience is typical. Nearly everyone who tries to figure out a next career takes a long time to find the one that is truly right. Most career transitions take about three years. It is rarely a linear path: We take two steps forward and one step back, and where we end up often surprises us.

Working Identity

Once we start questioning not just whether we are in the right job or organization today but also what we thought we wanted for the future, the job search methods we have all been taught fail us. But that doesn't mean we must resign ourselves to a random process governed by factors outside our control—a life crisis that forces us to reprioritize, an unexpected job offer. There is an alternative method that works according to a different logic than the plan-and-implement approach. Gary, Harris, and Susan, as well as many other successful career changers I have observed, shared this method, which I call the "test and learn" model of change. During times of transition—when our possible selves are shifting wildly—the only way to create change is by putting our possible identities into practice, working and crafting

TEST AND LEARN

Your working identity is an amalgam of the kind of work you do, the relationships and organizations that form part of your work life, and the story you tell about why you do what you do and how you arrived at that point. Reshaping that identity, therefore, is a matter of making adjustments to all three of those aspects over time. The adjustments happen tentatively and incrementally, so the process can seem disorderly. In fact, it is a logical process of testing, discovering, and adapting that can be learned by almost anyone seeking professional renewal.

Crafting experiments

Working identity is defined by what we do, the professional activities that engage us. ►	Try out new activities and professional roles on a small scale before making a major commitment to a different path.

Shifting connections

Working identity is also defined by the company we keep, our working relationships, and the professional groups to which we belong. ►	Develop contacts that can open doors to new worlds, and look for role models and new reference groups to guide and benchmark your progress.

Making sense

Working identity is also defined by the formative events in our lives and the stories that link who we were and who we will become. ►	Find or create catalysts and triggers for change, and use them as occasions to rework your life story.

them until they are sufficiently grounded in experience to guide more decisive steps. (See the sidebar "Test and Learn.")

The test-and-learn approach recognizes that the only way to counter uncertainty and resist the pull of the familiar is to make alternative futures more vivid, more tangible, and more doable. We acquired our old identities in practice. Likewise, we redefine them, in practice, by crafting experiments, shifting connections, and making sense of the changes we are going through. These three common practices lie at the heart of the most disparate of career changes, lending logic to what can look like chance occurrences and disorderly behavior.

Crafting Experiments

By far the biggest mistake people make when trying to change careers is delaying the first step until they have settled on a destination. This error is undermining because the only way we figure out what we really want to do is by giving it a try. Understandably, most people are reluctant to leap into the unknown. We must test our fantasies—otherwise, they remain just that. I discovered that most people create new working identities on the side at first, by getting involved in extracurricular ventures and weekend projects.

"Crafting experiments" refers to the practice of creating these side projects. Their great advantage is that we can try out new professional roles on a limited scale without compromising our current jobs or having to leap into new positions too quickly. In almost every instance of successful change that I have observed, the person had already been deeply engaged in the new career for quite some time.

There are many ways to set up experiments that work. Newly resolved to explore a range of possibilities, Susan took freelancing assignments in her old line of work and did pro bono work for charities as her lifeline to get her through this difficult period. Through that work, she began to develop contacts that led to paid charity consulting. Gradually, she became immersed in nonprofits, a sector she had never expected to find a career in. And she found herself enjoying freelancing. Today, she is working with the largest U.K. consulting firm that specializes in charities, and she has this to say: "All I hope is that I never again make the mistake of jumping before giving myself the chance to explore what I really want to do."

Other people use temporary assignments, outside contracts, advisory work, and moonlighting to get experience or build skills in new industries. Thanks to a temporary stint at the helm of his division, Harris got over his fear, which had silently plagued him for years, that he lacked the finance and cross-functional background necessary to be a good general manager. This concrete experience, more than any amount of self-reflection, helped him envision himself as a general manager. Taking courses or picking up training and credentials in a new area is still another way of experimenting. For many of the people in my study, an executive program, sabbatical, or extended vacation improved their capacity to move in a new direction. These breaks are powerful because they force us to step back from the daily routine while engaging us with new people and activities.

Shifting Connections

Consider how common it is for employees to say of their companies, "There is no one here I want to be like." At midcareer, our desire for change is rarely about only the work we do; it is perhaps more importantly about changing our working relationships so they are more satisfying and inspiring. "Shifting connections" refers to the practice of finding people who can help us see and grow into our new selves. For most successful career changers I have observed, a guiding figure or new professional community helped light the way and cushion the eventual leap.

Finding a new job always requires networking outside our usual circles. We get ideas and job leads by branching out. Gary, for example, used his alumni and company networks quite successfully. It was an ex-employee of his company—someone he didn't know personally—who got him the temporary project at his current company. But what clinched his decision, what made this job different from all the other conformist roles he had considered, was the opportunity to work for a role model he had long admired and from whom he could learn the ropes.

Seeking refuge in close working relationships is natural in times of change and uncertainty. But Harris made a classic mistake in turning to an old mentor, Alfred, who was too invested in Harris remaining the unsure protégé to give him room to grow. Harris's way out of this "codependent" relationship came via a person he had met casually at a professional conference. Gerry, the company founder who later hired Harris as his COO, initially approached Harris for regulatory advice. Eventually, they developed an informal consulting relationship. In Gerry, Harris found a person who believed in his potential as a general manager and offered a different kind of close, interdependent working relationship. "It was such a contrast to my relationship with Alfred," Harris says. "It's not as paternal. Gerry knows things I need to learn—things that relate to creative financing, ways to raise money—but he also needs to learn from me. He doesn't know how to run a company, and I do. He's looking to me to teach him what's necessary to develop an organization, to build a foundation. I think I can learn a lot from Gerry, but it's a more mature and more professional relationship than I had with Alfred."

To make a break with the past, we must venture into unknown networks—and not just for job leads. Often it is strangers who are best equipped to help us see who we are becoming.

Making Sense

In the middle of the confusion about which way to go, many of us hope for one event that will clarify everything, that will transform our stumbling moves into a coherent trajectory. Julio Gonzales, a doctor trying to leave the practice of medicine, put it like this: "I was waiting for an epiphany—I wake up in the middle of the night and the Angel of Mercy tells me *this* is what I should do." The third working identity practice, "making sense," refers to creating our own triggers for change: infusing events—the momentous and the mundane—with special meaning and weaving them into a story about who we are becoming.

Every person who has changed careers has a story about the moment of truth. For John Alexander, the would-be author I've mentioned, the moment of truth came when, on a whim, he visited an astrologer. To his surprise, the first thing she said to him was, "I'm glad I haven't been *you* for the last two or three years. You have been undergoing a painful internal tug-of-war between two opposing factions. One side wants stability, economic well-being, and social status, and the other craves artistic expression, maybe as a writer or an impresario. You may wish to believe that there can be reconciliation between these two. I tell you, there cannot be." Another career changer, a woman who had grown increasingly frustrated as an executive in a high-tech startup, said, "One day my husband just asked me, 'Are you happy? If you are, that's great. But you don't *look* happy.' His question prompted me to reconsider what I was doing."

It would be easy to believe from such accounts that career changes have their geneses in such moments. But the moment of insight is an effect, not a cause, of change. Across my many interviews, a striking discovery was that such moments tended to occur late in the transition process, only after much trial and tribulation. Rather than catalyzing change, defining moments helped people make sense of changes that had long been unfolding.

Trigger events don't just jolt us out of our habitual routines; they are the necessary pegs on which to hang our reinvention stories. Arranging life events into a coherent story is one of the subtlest, yet most demanding, challenges of career reinvention. To reinvent oneself is to rework one's story. At the start of a career transition, when all we have is a laundry list of diffuse ideas, it unsettles us that we have no story. It disturbs us to find so many different options appealing, and we worry that the same self who once chose what we no longer want to do might again make a bad choice. Without a story that explains why we must change, the external audience to whom we are selling our reinvention remains dubious, and we, too, feel unsettled and uncertain.

Good stories develop in the telling and retelling, by being put into the public sphere even before they are fully formed. Instead of being embarrassed about having visited an astrologer, for example, John told everyone his story and even wrote about it in a newspaper column. The closer he got to finding his creative outlet, the more the episode made sense and the less often his story elicited the "Why would you want to do that?" reaction. By making public declarations about what we seek and about the common thread that binds our old and new selves, we clarify our intentions and improve our ability to enlist others' support.

The Road Now Taken

Most of us know what we are trying to escape: the lockstep of a narrowly defined career, inauthentic or unstimulating work, numbing corporate politics, a lack of time for life outside of work. Finding an alternative that truly fits, like finding one's mission in life, cannot be accomplished overnight. It takes time, perseverance, and hard work. But effort isn't enough; a sound method and the skill to put it into practice are also required.

The idea of working one's identity flies in the face of everything we have always been told about choosing careers. It asks us to devote the greater part of our time and energy to action rather than reflection, to doing instead of planning. It tells us to give up the search for a 10-point plan and to accept instead a crooked path. But what appears to be a mysterious, road-to-Damascus process is actually a learning-by-doing practice that any of us can adopt. We start by taking action.

Herminia Ibarra is the Charles Handy Professor of Organizational Behavior at London Business School. She is the author of *Act Like a Leader, Think Like a Leader* (Harvard Business Review Press, 2015) and *Working Identity: Unconventional Strategies for Reinventing Your Career* (Harvard Business Review Press, 2003).

SECTION FOUR

Get Going

You've decided to make the switch! Hooray! Where to start? What's your first step? What details should you attend to? This section of the guide will help you broaden your network through informational interviews and quilt the different pieces of your educational and professional history into a comprehensive whole.

CHAPTER 10

Test-Drive Your Path

by Dorie Clark

It's impossible to know if you'll really like a career direction until you try it out. To avoid making costly mistakes—and wasting your energy—take a test-drive. Here, you'll read about people who apprenticed, volunteered, or job shadowed to discover their professional identities—and you'll learn how to find these experiences for yourself.

Apprenticing

Joanne Chang was swept into her first job when she graduated from Harvard in 1991. Because she'd majored

---

Reprinted from *HBR Guide to Getting the Right Job* (product #11737), Harvard Business Review Press, 2012.

in math and economics, "it seemed natural to go into investment banking or management consulting," she recalls. When a blue-chip management-consulting firm offered her a job, she grabbed it. But two years later—much of it spent on the road, advising companies spanning every industry from insurance to telecom—she knew it wasn't her calling.

She'd always been interested in cooking and baking—at Harvard, she'd been known as the Chocolate Chip Cookie Girl—so she decided to give that a try instead. "I sent a bunch of letters to chefs in town I didn't know, but I knew their reputation," she says. "I said, 'I have no formal training, but I love cooking and I'm interested in getting into the restaurant world, and I'll take any position.'"

Impressed with her chutzpah, intrigued by her résumé, and short an employee who had just left, Boston power chef Lydia Shire called Chang literally the next day and invited her for an interview. Chang got a job as a "bottom-of-the-ladder prep cook," tutored by a sous chef who "trained me and showed me recipes and what I needed to do—how to set up the station, what the dishes should look like." After three months, she worked her way up to her first job as a line cook.

The transition wasn't easy. "It's grimy, hard physical labor," she says. "It can be mundane—and there's a lot of stress." But she soon realized the food industry was where she wanted to be. "I remember clearly telling one of my consulting friends how exciting it was to be surrounded by people who were passionate about their work. When you cook, you're not making any money, so when you do it, it's with people who are there because they love cooking." And her work in the kitchen had a clear, direct impact. "You make a terrine, you slice it up, put it on a plate, and the server comes back and says they loved the terrine. It was an immediate gratification I hadn't had up to that point in my career."

Today, Chang is the impresario behind Flour—a chain of seven acclaimed bakeries in the Boston area—and a co-owner (with her husband, Christopher Myers) of the upscale Asian restaurant Myers + Chang. Now she's on the other side of the equation, hiring (as Lydia Shire did) people of all ages wanting to break into the restaurant industry—and she's more convinced than ever that apprenticeships are critical. "There are misconceptions about what it's like to be in the food business," says Chang. "It's imperative to spend some time working in the field before making a jump."

Volunteering

If you can spare your nights and weekends—or do without a paycheck for a short period—try volunteering as a way to illuminate possibilities. As executive coach Rebecca Zucker points out, volunteering "allows you to network with a new group of people in your target area. It allows you to keep your skill set fresh or build a new skill set. It's something you can put on a résumé—and it shows your commitment to a particular path." Zucker recalls one client who wanted to break into clean tech— a popular career in Silicon Valley that was hard to get started in without previous experience. "He volunteered to do research for a private equity firm on a certain niche within clean tech," she says. "Not only did he learn a ton and have something to put on his résumé, but it was also instrumental in helping him get a job in the field."

Deborah Shah had a similarly valuable experience volunteering in state politics. She'd always enjoyed politics but strictly as an observer: "I would typically watch the morning shows on Sunday, read the morning paper—I knew what was going on in the world but not as an insider." After feeling especially moved by a gubernatorial candidate's speech, she decided to get involved in his campaign. She showed up at headquarters and was given the most basic grunt work: making phone calls to voters. But she earned trust—and greater responsibility—because she was "the phone banker who showed up every day." Eventually, the campaign asked her to organize a senate district, then another, and Shah finally became a regional field director. She worked on the campaign for 11 months, unpaid, but in the process she discovered a passion: "I was interested in persuading people to vote. I really liked campaigning."

After the campaign ended, she learned something else: She'd made a name for herself. A state representative she'd met on the trail was headed for a special election and wanted her to run his campaign. When she helped him win, other calls poured in. In the past five years, she's headed races for governor, state senator, city councillor, and U.S. senator.

Volunteering can be beneficial even within your own company. New York–based coach Alisa Cohn suggests stepping up for committees that will allow you to build connections in different departments. "You can volunteer for any press function or global committee. It might feel thankless, but what you're getting is a broader network and the experience of doing something different. It's especially good if you feel like you've been boxed in or pigeonholed. If you're in engineering or finance and you want to get more experience in marketing or strategic planning, they can't stop you, because you're volunteering."

Volunteering also helps you find out what you don't want to do. The summer after I graduated from college—thinking a career in public relations sounded exciting—I landed at a boutique PR firm in Washington, D.C., that specialized in education issues. By test-driving the field with an entry-level job—which consisted largely of cold-calling disinterested reporters—I learned that PR was not where I wanted to end up.

Job Shadowing

Occasionally, a day working in a field is all it takes. One coach recalls a web designer client who "liked design but couldn't stand spending five days a week in front of the computer." Looking for a creative career that included more interaction with people, she became interested in floral design and read about it extensively. She did 10 informational interviews in the field and, convinced it was right for her, agreed to her coach's suggestion to shadow someone for a day. "At the end of the morning," the coach remembers, "she had three questions: Is the room always cold? Is the floor always cement? And are you always on your feet? And the guy said, 'The room is always cold because we have to keep the flowers fresh, the floor is cement because I'm dropping wet flowers on it, and I'm always on my feet because we're moving around and delivering flowers.' And that was the end of that."

For those who'd like more immersion—or whose dream jobs aren't located nearby—there's Vocation Vacations, a company that allows participants to test-drive more than 125 careers. Say you'd like to be an alpaca rancher. If you don't know any personally, you can pay $849, head to Oregon, and work side by side with a real-life ranch mentor for two days.

If you want to make any kind of professional leap—even if it's to something less esoteric, like becoming a freelance writer—it's essential to do your "personal and professional due diligence," says Vocation Vacations founder Brian Kurth. "It's doing your homework and getting questions answered that you didn't know you needed to ask," he says. "One question I always have clients ask mentors is 'What do you know now that you didn't know when you launched your business?' The goal is for the clients not to make the same mistakes—to hit the road faster."

Work for Free If You Can

Life is not fair. One shining example of that is the fact that you'll probably get the best opportunities if you work for free. It's not always necessary—Joanne Chang got hired as a paid prep cook and received on-the-job training. But let's be clear: Without experience, you'll be starting at the bottom and making a meager salary even if you are remunerated. (See the sidebar "Set Goals for Your Career Experiment.")

SET GOALS FOR YOUR CAREER EXPERIMENT

by Bill Barnett

Experimenting with a new career can be exhilarating. To make the most of your career experiments, think like a research scientist and know what you hope to learn. The more explicit you are about your learning objectives, the more you'll be able to determine if a potential career path is the one for you.

To help clarify what you hope to learn from your experiment, set goals and document your ideas and expectations. Consider these sample questions:

- *The purpose:* What do you hope to accomplish in this field? What do people do in their day-to-day jobs? Does it match your interests?

- *Skill level:* How do you see yourself stacking up against peers? Does the prospect of achieving true mastery in that line of work excite you? Can you imagine advancing into a leadership position?

- *The culture:* How is performance rated? What is the level of teamwork? How do people communicate? Are there any ethical issues in the field?

- *The lifestyle:* How intense is the work? How many hours per week will you be working? Is travel involved?

(continued)

SET GOALS FOR YOUR CAREER EXPERIMENT

Review what you've written every week or so. Evaluate what you're learning and what more you need to discover.

The best way to learn from the experiment is to treat it seriously. Success will help you decide if it's the right field for you, and it might lead directly to a job offer. Success will also help you build a network and a record of accomplishment, as well as develop any skills you may need if you take a different career path.

But beware of too much experimentation. Testing new directions can be seductive—a way to do things while putting off tough decisions. Don't get too comfortable. Experiment, learn what you need, and then decide.

Bill Barnett led the strategy practice at McKinsey & Company and has taught career strategy to graduate students at Yale University and Rice University. He now applies business strategy concepts to careers. He is the author of *The Strategic Career: Let Business Principles Guide You* (Stanford Business Books, 2015).

Adapted from content posted on hbr.org, July 13, 2012.

There's an upside, though: You may have a better opportunity to gain meaningful skills if you work for free because once employers start forking over cash, they often want grunt work for their money. If you're working gratis, your employer can afford to deploy you on long-range, strategic projects that wouldn't otherwise get done.

I certainly had that experience during my college internship days. When I worked for free at a D.C.-based advocacy group, my boss toted me along to key meetings and let me work on substantive research projects. The following two summers, I was incredibly proud to be hired for elite paid internship programs (at the aforementioned PR firm in D.C. and at a New York City–based advertising agency). But as I endured an endless array of menial assignments, it felt as if they wanted to soak me for every minute their five dollars an hour could buy. I made about $3,000 each summer—enough to pay rent—but I learned a lot less.

Dorie Clark is a marketing strategist and professional speaker who teaches at Duke University's Fuqua School of Business. She is the author of *Entrepreneurial You* (Harvard Business Review Press, 2017), *Stand Out* (Portfolio, 2015), and *Reinventing You* (Harvard Business Review Press, 2013).

CHAPTER 11

Research Your Destination with Informational Interviews

by Dorie Clark

Informational interviews with friends of friends, school and workplace alumni, and others in professions you're considering will help you explore career options and make connections. They provide a safe environment to ask pointed questions—which allows you to find promising possibilities and weed out choices that aren't a good fit.

Reprinted from *HBR Guide to Getting the Right Job* (product #11737), Harvard Business Review Press, 2012.

But there's a risk: If you don't make a good first impression at an informational interview, you can torpedo the relationship. You may not know at this point exactly where you're headed, and that's OK. But as San Francisco–based executive coach Rebecca Zucker notes, "You still need to come across in a way that inspires confidence and makes other people want to help you." Here's how to do that.

Step 1: Be Clear About the Help You're Asking For

When you aren't totally sure what you want, it may seem like a good strategy to leave yourself wide open. For example, you might say, "I'd like something in communications." But what kind of communications? Marketing? Advertising? Public relations? For a nonprofit? A big corporation? In health care? Consumer products? If you haven't even begun to focus your search, it becomes a monumental task—and a waste of time—for people to assist you.

Zucker suggests creating a brief "positioning statement" before you start to make your inquiries. "It can be tentative," she says, "but it should still be confident: 'I'm looking to make a change, and I'm not sure what direction I'm heading, but two things that intrigue me are X and Y.' Put it out in an organized manner that people can respond to and that will add to your research."

If you aren't sure what you want, or you're interested in more than one potential career, just be as specific as you can for now. This will expand your options, not limit them. Somebody may say, for instance, "I don't know anyone in New England archaeology, but if you

MASTERING THE COLD CALL

It's a lot easier to reach out to people who have some connection to you, even a tenuous one ("I'm calling at the suggestion of Phil, your former coworker"). But what if you don't have any connections in your chosen field? Take a page from Elizabeth Amini, who runs an online startup.

After finishing college with a cognitive science degree, Amini—who'd intended to become a surgeon—discovered during a hospital internship that medicine was a bad fit for her. Using skills she'd developed working at her college newspaper, she started her own graphic design company. She eventually landed a consulting project—and then a full-time job—at NASA. But after several years, she realized she didn't want to make it a career. So, at 30, she quit her job and set out to find her next move. "I felt really lost," she recalls. "All my friends who were also premed had graduated from medical school and were practicing, and here I was, not knowing what career direction I should take."

Amini made a list of five professions that intrigued her: nonprofit management, art curation, real estate development, management consulting, and international business development. And then she did her research. Her goal was to gather 5 to 10 "data points" for each field. These are the steps she followed:

1. *Choose your target companies.* Based in Los Angeles, Amini decided to focus on professionals

(continued)

MASTERING THE COLD CALL

she could meet in person. Using the website www.infousa.com (you could also use various library databases), she created a list of the largest firms in her city in each of her target industries.

2. *Identify the right executives.* Next, she searched online to find the right people to talk to: She typed in names of companies, along with phrases like "international business vice president." Then she checked dates of news articles, press releases, and so on to make sure the people she found were still in these roles. And she tried to glean other salient information (for instance, that an executive was heading up an expansion into South America).

3. *Research the contact points.* Amini looked up the companies' press offices and investor relations departments online to deduce their standard email patterns (such as john.doe@company.com). She also dug around for preferred nicknames. "When the name is Michael," she says, "search on the web to see if he goes by 'Michael' or 'Mike.' Otherwise, the administrative assistant is going to think, Nobody calls him that—you probably don't know him." She then called the companies' main lines after hours to

get voicemail directories and learn the executives' extensions.

4. ***Avoid the gatekeeper.*** Armed with this information, she was finally ready to make her move. She could email or—even better—call. "When you call and ask for an extension number directly, people never question why you're calling the way they do if you ask for someone by name," she says. They're more likely to put you right through. Also, she recommends calling just before or just after business hours, when the assistants may not be at their desks—but the executives may be around. "Assistants are there to screen you out, so you want to avoid them as much as possible," she says.

5. ***Start at the top—but not the very top.*** "If you really want to learn what an industry's like, you have to talk to seasoned veterans," Amini says. She suggests starting with the COO's office— "because that assistant knows everybody." The goal isn't to score interviews with COOs; it's to get their imprimatur: "You can say to the assistant, 'I know the COO is probably not the right person to talk to, but who is your best salesperson' (or marketing person, or whomever you need to reach)? And then when you call those

(continued)

MASTERING THE COLD CALL

people, you can say the COO's office recommended them."

6. ***Make the right ask.*** Don't request an hour of someone's time, or even a half hour. Busy executives aren't going to crack open their calendars for someone they have no real connection to. Instead, warm them up with context—let them know that you've read one of their books, for example. Then tell them, "I was impressed by XYZ, and I'd like to ask you some questions about how you became so successful. Is it possible to schedule a 10-minute phone call? Or, if you're free, I'd be happy to take you to lunch." Most people will opt for the phone call—which seems easy compared with lunch.

7. ***Schedule smartly.*** Many professionals' schedules are heavily booked for the next few weeks— so if you ask for a slot "in the next week or two," you're likely to get turned down. And if you ask to connect "sometime this year," your request won't seem urgent. Even if people agree to meet with you, they may eventually brush you off. Amini suggests asking to meet "this month or next," when unscheduled blocks are probably still available.

8. ***Don't get discouraged.*** Some executives tried to dodge her requests, but Amini persevered. "One guy said I needed to talk to someone more junior, so I said, 'I'd like insight from the most successful person in the department, and that's you.'" That line won him over. Another person— in real estate development—screamed, "I don't have time to talk to some #*$@ student! I'm up to my neck in lawsuits!" and hung up on her. "To me," Amini says, "that's a data point. I got the same information I would have in a 10-minute interview."

9. ***Pounce on opportunities.*** When browsing the *Forbes* 500, Amini read about a billionaire real estate mogul who lived in Los Angeles. She called after 5:30 p.m. and got him on the phone—"and, oddly," she recalls, "he agreed to lunch." She was thrilled with the opportunity, but shortly after she got off the phone, she panicked. "I said, 'Pick your favorite place,' but then I thought, Where do billionaires go for lunch? What if lunch is $1,000?" She decided to proceed, despite the risks: I'll put it on my credit card, she thought, and if it's more than my rent, I'll find a way to pay it off. The mogul took her to

(continued)

MASTERING THE COLD CALL

a local deli—his favorite spot—and lunch for two came to $17. He spent 90 minutes with her and outlined "what it took to be him."

Today, Amini isn't working in any of the five fields she explored in her informational interviews. (Harkening back to her premed days, her startup focuses on cutting-edge brain research.) But she learned invaluable lessons from the process. The real estate mogul told her that "he goes on vacation with his family for six weeks, and he turns off his cell phone and laptop entirely. He said that whatever falls apart in your business during that time is good, because you can see what parts of your business don't work without you." For Amini, that was a revelation: "I'm only going on vacation for a week, and I'm not a billionaire." She could disconnect, too, and the world could wait. "You end up with all these random lessons that are important," she says, "even if the person's field is not relevant to you in the end."

like historic preservation, I know someone who works at the Victorian Society." You want to paint a picture so clear that your contacts will think of real-life people they know who can help you. (See the sidebar "Mastering the Cold Call.")

Executive coach Michael Melcher also emphasizes the importance of being up-front about your motives for meeting. "It's an error to call up a former client, say you want to catch up, and then when you get together, spring on them that 'the reason I want to talk to you is that I, too, want to be an entertainment lawyer.' It's insincere." Instead, he suggests an opening along these lines: "'I'd like to get together, and I have an ulterior motive: I'm exploring a transition to XYZ, and I'd like to ask you questions about it.' That way, they can say yes or no—and they'll probably say yes."

Step 2: Read Up Before You Meet

Do some research on your contact's company and industry before you meet. By making a timely remark about a new product release, for example, or asking about the impact of some proposed regulation on the industry, you can show that you're well informed and create a bond.

Melcher says to consider the "highest and best use" of the person you're interviewing. He's frequently contacted by people who want to become executive coaches. "What I won't do anymore is talk to people who say, 'I'm wondering where I can go for coaching training.' I feel like that's public information; they can look online." He's much more willing to help them choose between competing options, for example, or examine revenue models for a new coaching practice. "You want to show that you've done your homework—that you've taken it as far as possible before talking with the person," he advises.

Step 3: Make It Convenient for the Interviewee

Let's face it: You're asking for people's time, so you want to make it very convenient for them. Invite them to pick the date, time, and location—and pay for their drink or meal. I've heard friends who are unemployed grouse about spending money to take out folks who are earning a healthy paycheck—which is exactly the wrong perspective. It's probably costing them hundreds of dollars in lost productivity to meet with you. So pick up the check.

Arrive when you say you will, and don't take up too much time. Karen Landolt—a former lawyer who switched fields and now heads up a career services office at a state university—estimates she's invited well over a hundred contacts out on informational interviews in the past decade. "If people say they have 20 minutes, I'll keep track. I'll say, 'It's been 20 minutes. If you have more time, I have more questions—but if not, I want to respect your time.'"

Step 4: Ask the Right Questions

Good questions reflect a basic understanding of the field and a focus on the interviewee's own experiences. Career counselor Phyllis Stein, formerly the director of Radcliffe Career Services at Harvard University, suggests the following:

- What is your typical day like? Your typical week? (And if there's no such thing, ask about the most recent day or week.)

- What do you like most about your job? What do you like the least?

- What does it take to be successful in this field? In this company?

- I'm planning the following steps (name them) toward obtaining a job in this field. Have I overlooked any strategy or resource you think might be helpful?

Step 5: Leave with Other Names

You can learn from salespeople here: Ask interviewees who else you should connect with in their company or field, and see if they'd be willing to make introductions. And check LinkedIn to see if they have connections to other marketers, Comcast employees, specialists in Argentinean culture—whatever types of contacts you're looking for.

When you're trying to make connections, don't forget to tap your alumni network, whether it's from college, grad school, or former employers. Recalls Landolt, the former lawyer: "When I was making a transition, I was at a huge firm with 450 attorneys and a turnover rate of about 70%. There were attorneys all over who had worked there, and I used the network, because we'd been through the same war. We didn't know each other, but I'd talk to current employees at the firm and ask, 'Can you introduce us?' And they'd say sure."

Step 6: Keep the Connection Alive

You'll want to turn informational interviews into ongoing relationships, so look for key details you can follow up on later. Maybe the person you're meeting with just got back from a vacation to Fiji, or you both like the Dodgers, or your kids go to the same school. That's your starting point. Then after you've sent the all-important thank-you note (it does make an impact), you can forward interesting travel articles, send an email when your team makes the playoffs, or invite your contact to sit with you at the school fundraiser. With each interaction, strive to learn more about the person to add depth to the relationship. The process of learning someone's hometown, college, names and ages of children, favorite hobbies, favorite restaurants, previous jobs, and long-range goals provides a raft of opportunities to connect over shared interests and keep up a dialogue.

Periodically report back on your career development so the folks who have given you counsel can see that you're applying their advice. "Make it an open feedback channel," says executive coach Rebecca Zucker. "Let them know, 'Here are some of the things I learned, and I'd love to talk more with you as I progress.'"

Elizabeth Amini, the online entrepreneur featured in the sidebar "Mastering the Cold Call," suggests getting in touch around major milestones. "You can send holiday greetings ('Thank you for your mentoring this year') and updates on advice they gave you ('Thanks for recommending the University of Southern California—I applied and just got in')." Put reminders in your calendar to touch base.

Step 7: Add Value to the Relationship

Just as your contacts are helping you, try to add value to their lives by providing helpful connections of your own or simply offering encouragement.

For example, I make a point of congratulating people when I see they've been quoted in an article. In the wake of the 2004 Asian tsunami, Elizabeth Amini made $10 donations in the names of those who'd helped her out and sent them a short note letting them know. "It wasn't calculated at all," she says, "but people were so thankful."

Conducting a slew of informational interviews might sound stressful, but you can actually enjoy the process if you keep it in perspective. When Karen Landolt felt demoralized in her job as a corporate lawyer, these conversations gave her something to look forward to. "It was almost therapeutic and how I got through my days: At least I get to have lunch with this interesting person."

Dorie Clark is a marketing strategist and professional speaker who teaches at Duke University's Fuqua School of Business. She is the author of *Entrepreneurial You* (Harvard Business Review Press, 2017), *Stand Out* (Portfolio, 2015), and *Reinventing You* (Harvard Business Review Press, 2013).

CHAPTER 12

Change Your Career Without Having to Start All Over Again

by Dorie Clark

The thought of giving up hard-earned seniority and starting over at the bottom is often too demoralizing for those of us experienced professionals who'd like to make a career transition. But there are ways you can shift jobs or even careers without giving up your professional status. Instead, you can work creatively to transfer it, so that even if you're starting in a completely different field,

---

Adapted from content posted on hbr.org, May 24, 2016 (product #H02WEN).

you'll benefit from your years of labor. Here are four ways to capitalize on your past experience.

Take Advantage of the Halo Effect

Since the early 1920s, researchers have understood that people are generally susceptible to the "halo effect": viewing others as being totally good and competent, or totally bad and incompetent (minus any shades of gray), based on an initial evaluation of the person. Often, this can lead to heuristic errors and people's true abilities being overlooked. But if you're an experienced professional, you might as well use this human quirk to your advantage.

Recognize that if you've proven to be successful in one field, others are likely to view you as being excellent all around and therefore a great candidate in another field. For example, look to the political success of actors like Arnold Schwarzenegger or the business success of sports heroes like famed skateboarder Tony Hawk.

Make Use of Your Assets

If you're an experienced professional, you've likely accrued two benefits that younger reinventers may not have: connections and money. Take stock of the particular advantages you possess, and think about how you can use them. If you've built up a nest egg, you may be able to take time off to volunteer at a high level for a cause you believe in, gaining valuable experience and paving the way to a paid job offer.

Even if you're transitioning away from the field where you made your name, your contacts may well have relationships with top performers in other industries they can introduce you to. In any city, the most successful professionals are likely to know one another through clubs and charity events. Find out—through LinkedIn and casual conversations—who your friends know in your desired industry, and who they might be willing to introduce you to.

Your existing contacts can also help your transition by serving as wingmen who will sing your praises to the new communities you're interacting with and allay any concerns about the transferability of your skills. Someone might wonder whether a former financier could make it as a nonprofit executive director, for instance. But if your friend forcefully defends your passion for the cause and your people skills, you're very likely to at least win an interview for the position.

Find Opportunities Where Inexperience Is a Virtue

You might suspect that people would be reluctant to hire someone at a high level who lacks experience in the field. And in general, you'd be right. But there are certain exceptions. If a company is in trouble—the established ways of doing business haven't been working for them—they're often unusually receptive to hiring an unconventional candidate as a leader. Outsiders without industry experience are risky choices that could crash and burn. But according to the research of Harvard Business School professor Gautam Mukunda, they're also disproportionately likely to be the best leaders, who can resurrect troubled companies, map out bold new strategic directions, or guide a nascent startup to dominance.

If you make that case forcefully—and can explain why your inexperience in their field is more than compensated for by the skills you've gained in your previous career—you may suddenly become a very desirable candidate. When I was hired early in my career as the executive director of a bicycling advocacy nonprofit, my cycling knowledge was so lackluster, I couldn't even remember what brand of bicycle I owned. But, I argued to the board, I brought media, lobbying, and communication skills the organization didn't have at the time—and they ultimately agreed and hired me.

No one wants to feel that their years of hard work have been wasted. If the thought of losing your professional status and having to start from scratch has been dissuading you from considering a professional reinvention, think again. With these three strategies, you can build on the best parts of your experience while transitioning into your next chapter.

Dorie Clark is a marketing strategist and professional speaker who teaches at Duke University's Fuqua School of Business. She is the author of *Entrepreneurial You* (Harvard Business Review Press, 2017), *Stand Out* (Portfolio, 2015), and *Reinventing You* (Harvard Business Review Press, 2013).

CHAPTER 13

Turning Your Complex Career Path into a Coherent Story

by Anna Ranieri

It's hard when you've had a nonstandard career trajectory and you want to reenter the workforce, move to a higher position, or enter a new field. Will a marketing firm see you as a good leadership candidate if you've always been a professional fund-raiser and small-business owner? Would a medical devices company view you as capable of learning their product line if you've worked in the automobile or hospitality industries? Will a corporate hiring manager take you seriously if you've spent the

Adapted from content posted on hbr.org, August 14, 2015 (product #H027ZV).

past 10 years mostly volunteering? In these cases, you may not be the slam-dunk candidate. But you're more likely to persuade an enlightened hiring manager, venture funder, or board member if you can articulate how all of your varied experiences and skills actually make you a better candidate than the conventional applicant.

How do you do that? You tell your story in a way that connects the dots. Unlike a more typical candidate, you have to assure that your audience can identify the thread that runs through your career narrative and make sense of your varied skills, training, experiences, and choices.

Identify Themes

For others to understand your trajectory, you have to first make sense of it yourself. Identify the themes that run through your professional life. This will take some concentration and reflection. In fact, it may be something that a longtime friend, colleague, or family member identifies before you do. Some examples:

- "You've always liked building things, ever since you got a set of wooden blocks for your first birthday."

- "You never settle for the status quo. No matter where you've worked and what you've done, you've always looked to create something new."

- "You motivate people, whether you're running the PTA, leading a team at work, or finding people to join the town council."

Not long ago I recognized a coherent theme in my working life, and I've shared it with my career-coaching clients as an example of how to capture a personal story. I'd taken Latin all through high school and loved translating the ancient tale of "The Aeneid" into something resembling modern English. I majored in literature in college, reading in Italian and French. I almost accepted a job as a translator after I got my degree, but took a position as a fund-raiser for my university instead. I went to business school a few years later and then worked in marketing. Soon after I returned to institutional development (the uptown name for fund-raising) while getting degrees in counseling and psychology. When I finished my PhD, I continued my private practice but also added career counseling and executive coaching to my professional mix.

Told like that, it seems like a trail of somewhat disconnected experiences. But what ties it all together is the process of translating: translating a text from one language to another, translating the significance of an academic program to a potential donor, translating the benefits of a product to consumers, translating a client's concerns into possible ways forward, and helping clients translate their own feelings, thoughts, and capabilities to others. Eureka!

Ask yourself: What are the kinds of tasks that I like to do? Consider the processes and activities you've enjoyed most in school or at work and as a volunteer, family member, or friend. Think about or ask others what may tie these interests together. Without a nod to a specific position or title, you may find that the general motif is being an effective listener, building relationships, solving complex problems, rethinking standard ways of operating, creating a new vision, or motivating people to take action. This is what you've most enjoyed and therefore tend to do well, because you've spent time at it. This theme that emerges from your experience may tie together a wide variety of activities with a common thread that unites them all.

Create and Rehearse Your Story

Once you've identified your own theme, the next step is to tell your story. Craft it, and take any opportunity to share it with those who can help advance your career: hiring managers, funders, colleagues, publicists, or the acquaintance you meet at a networking event or a local barbecue.

Forget titles, positions, and industries. Focus on what you're best at, using terms that pull together your diverse experiences, those seemingly unrelated industries, and the serendipitous opportunities you've had to learn something new. Don't be humble: Leave off the "Well, I've never done exactly this before, but . . . " Instead, say with confidence, "Here's what I do well."

A few examples:

- "I'm a relationship builder, and I've always been commended for my ability to listen to people's needs and help craft a solution for them."

- "Complex problem solving is exciting to me. I love to delve into thorny problems, work hard at teasing out the issues at hand, and get to the heart of the matter."

- "I thrive on creative thinking, whether I'm coming up with a new product or a new way of working.

It's impossible for me to settle for the status quo when I see that my team can create something better."

You can talk about previously held positions or companies later. First, establish the theme you want your audience to understand before they get stuck wondering, "But does he or she have enough time/experience/training?" You've connected the dots so they don't have to.

This theme can then become your proverbial calling card. Include it:

- At the top of your résumé, at the beginning of your elevator pitch, and in your descriptions to recruiters and in job interviews

- In your pitch to possible funders, your marketing materials, and conversational openers

- In your request to your boss for a promotion

After all, you want to ensure that others understand your competencies and the crystal clear rationale for your landing that job, that funding, or that promotion. You can't expect anyone else to do that for you: You have to connect the dots.

———————————

Anna Ranieri is an executive coach, career counselor, and speaker. She is the coauthor of *How Can I Help? What You Can (and Can't) Do to Counsel a Friend, Colleague, or Family Member with a Problem* (CreateSpace, 2012).

CHAPTER 14

Use Your LinkedIn Profile to Power a Career Transition

by Jane Heifetz

We all know the power of LinkedIn for job hunting and networking. But how do we use it to help *change* careers—to make sure we're found by the right recruiters, hiring managers, colleagues—not ones from our past, but from our future careers?

It's tempting to create an "everything but the kitchen sink" profile that makes you look qualified for both the job you have and the one you want. But that'll just confuse your readers and send them running—to others' LinkedIn pages. Instead, focus your profile on your new

---

Adapted from content posted on hbr.org, May 28, 2015 (product #H023XV).

career direction, just as you've tailored your résumé to specific jobs. In both cases, highlight your most relevant experiences, and minimize or omit the rest. Here's how to do that on LinkedIn.

Headline

Focus first on your headline. LinkedIn autopopulates this field with your current position, but don't let it. Instead, use the 120 characters to write your own eye-catching headline. Why is this so important? If I'm searching for someone like you on LinkedIn, my search results will reveal only your name and headline—and I could easily overlook you. But if you write an irresistible headline, I'll take the time to click to your entire profile.

Let's look at how one midcareerist uses her distinctive headline to attract the right people and opportunities.

Kristi Sullivan has been a successful marketing executive for more than 15 years. While still very committed to her current marketing VP role, she also wants to add a new direction to her career path: marketing small businesses in the health and wellness industry. She is also a devoted yoga practitioner and instructor. So this is her two-part headline: *Holistic health/yoga instructor, consultant, connector. Marketing executive for small businesses and nonprofits.*

Kristi immediately distinguishes herself from other marketers by putting health and yoga first. And she attracts people who need help with their holistic health and yoga businesses.

Check to see how distinctive your headline is by searching LinkedIn for people like you. Kristi found lots of marketing executives but no one else with holistic health and yoga in their headlines—a very good sign.

Summary

Now that your headline has attracted the right people, keep them reading. Tell a compelling story, and write it in the first person (more on storytelling in chapter 13). Unlike a résumé, your LinkedIn summary gives you much more space (up to 2,000 characters) to highlight past accomplishments and connect them to what you want to do next.

This is especially important if you've changed careers before. Craft a cohesive narrative that pulls together what might otherwise appear to be fragmented pieces of your professional past. This will prevent your profile reader from wondering what the heck you're trying to do *now*—or why you appear scattered and unfocused.

Here's how Kristi accomplishes this. She stitches together three areas of her professional and personal endeavors: marketing small businesses and nonprofits, women's business success, holistic health/yoga instruction and business consultant. She hooks her profile readers with this opening statement: *I am devoted to and excel in three areas, with each area strengthening the others: marketing small businesses and nonprofits, promoting women's business success, and holistic health and yoga instructor and business consultant. Let me expand a bit on each.*

She makes it easy for readers to quickly skim her summary by including headers that call out each of those three areas. And she introduces each area with a sentence that ties it to the others. For example, she connects her Women's Business Success section to the economic development work she's been doing for the past 15 years: *Because I'm passionate about enabling women to make positive differences in the workplace and the economy at large, I launched the Farmington Valley chapter of BIG (Believe, Inspire, Grow).*

And then in the Holistic Health/Yoga Instructor and Consultant section, she makes connections to her work in economic development and women's business by noting: *I see holistic health as a critical component of individuals', organizations', and communities' well-being.*

Finally, she ends her summary with an invitation to specific types of people: *I'm always interested in hearing from holistic-health business owners and female entrepreneurs, as well as economic-development professionals. Please contact me via InMail.*

Experience

Once you've nailed your headline and summary, tailor each of the positions in your Experience section. Here's how:

- **Write in the first person** to provide continuity with your first-person summary.

- **Focus on accomplishments,** not responsibilities, as you would in any résumé or profile. But highlight only the accomplishments that are most relevant to the new type of work you're seeking. Make those accomplishments concrete by noting the problem you solved, how you solved it, and the specific results you generated.

Here's an example of how Kristi focuses on some of her most relevant accomplishments: fund-raising, client acquisition, and social media: *I've brought in close to $1 million in new funding and more than 20 new clients. I established a Connecticut nonprofit's presence on Facebook, Twitter, LinkedIn, and YouTube, growing its followers by 150% in the first year. I also conceived an e-newsletter, blog, and vlog to enhance its social media presence and website.*

Recommendations

Sparingly add recommendations to selected positions— the ones most relevant to the new type of work you're seeking. Invite one or two people to recommend you. And don't hesitate to direct their testimonials: You'll make it easier and faster for them and more effective for you. Tell them exactly the types of positions you're now targeting and the skills you'd like them to highlight.

Images and Media Samples

Use images and media samples to draw attention to your most impressive accomplishments and add them only to the positions you want your new profile readers to focus on. For example, Kristi added her colorful business card to her summary section, a video screenshot and link to her presentation about internal social media strategies, and a photo of her teaching yoga on a stand-up paddleboard.

When you're trying to get into a new line of work, you have to prove that you possess the skills it will take to be successful in a different role. With a targeted profile that catches readers' attention, you'll position yourself well to make that change.

———————

Jane Heifetz is the founder and principal of Right Résumés and a contributing editor to *Harvard Business Review*.

CHAPTER 15

A Scorecard to Help You Compare Two Jobs

by Allison Rimm

You have a big career decision to make. Maybe you've been offered an exciting new opportunity on the other side of the country. Or maybe you've been unhappy in your job and need a change but haven't been able to find inspiring alternatives.

Several of the professionals I've coached share a common struggle: how to make major decisions that balance career growth with satisfaction in other domains of their lives. While it's often easy to see the impact a certain choice will have on objective criteria such as duties,

Adapted from content posted on hbr.org, April 20, 2015 (product #H03MBN).

position, prestige, salary, and opportunities for advancement, evaluating the "softer" considerations is tougher. But things like cultural fit, the quality of interactions with colleagues, the ability to exert influence, and the impact on family and social life all deeply affect how personally satisfied someone feels with their work.

To help my clients take an objective look at decidedly subjective considerations, I've developed a tool that allows them to quantify and visualize the pros and cons of various choices, taking into consideration the impact each would have on matters of both heart and head.

Here's how I used it with a physician I'll call Dinesh. He was feeling stuck trying to decide whether he should continue working in his current position at a prestigious academic medical center, which he truly enjoyed, or accept an exciting leadership position at a nearby community hospital. Dinesh was weighing some pretty standard "head" issues of salary, resources, leadership potential, commute, and call schedules. But he knew this was a huge change and needed to evaluate the more feelings-based issues such as how much he would enjoy his new colleagues, whether he would have the flexibility to manage his workload, and whether he could prioritize time with his family. Some of his "heart" issues also included his self-image as it related to "just" being a busy, highly regarded clinician as opposed to being seen as a leader with broader influence beyond his own patient care responsibilities.

We started by listing all the factors he was considering and the relative importance of each, on a scale of 1 to 5, so that Dinesh could see how they related to one another (see table 15-1). Under the "current hospital" and the "new hospital" headings is the score he assigned each choice regarding how good it would be for each factor, again rated on a scale of 1 to 5. We then multiplied the ratings by importance and added the total for each factor to derive a weighted total score for each job option.

A very interesting thing happened. While the "current hospital" job scored higher overall, viewing the scores in this way made it possible to see that the relative downsides of the new job were likely temporary. Even though it confirmed his gut feeling that his day-to-day life in the short term was better at his current job, his potential for career growth over the long haul was greatly enhanced by taking the job at the community hospital. The issues that decreased quality of life at the community hospital were mainly related to workload, protected time, and flexibility of schedule—considerations that would likely have a negative impact on his family life. He also realized that a promotion of this magnitude would be very unlikely to happen in his home institution. By having a tool that allowed him to visualize the relative impact of each factor, he was able to see that he'd likely be better off at the community hospital after the first year once he'd finished recruiting new physicians who could share the workload. This was a concept that was hard to grasp by just thinking things through without a structured framework.

Another client, whom I'll call Martha, had always been in management and needed a change from her current position. She was looking at executive roles in other organizations as well as fund-raising opportunities but wasn't getting jazzed about any of these options.

TABLE 15-1

A career decision scorecard

This example involves a physician choosing between his current job and a new role.

Decision factor	Importance weight	CURRENT HOSPITAL		NEW HOSPITAL	
		Decision factor score (1–5)	Combined score (importance weight × decision factor score)	Decision factor score (1–5)	Combined score (importance weight × decision factor score)
Leadership opportunities	5	1	5	5	25
Ability to implement new programs	5	2	10	5	25
Salary	5	4	20	5	25
Flexible schedule	5	5	25	4	20
Workload	5	5	25	3	15
Potential influence across hospital	5	2	10	5	25
Protected academic time	5	5	25	2	10

Time in teaching rounds	5	5	25	2	10
Medical school appointment	5	5	25	3	15
Work on quality committee	5	5	25	5	25
Quality of coworkers	5	5	25	3	15
Work with fellows	2	2	4	2	4
Work with residents	2	2	4	2	4
Work with medical students	2	2	4	1	2
Commute	2	4	8	5	10
Total score			240		230

I suggested she complete a decision grid comparing the options she was currently considering. The results surprised us both: Looking at the completed grid, she could plainly see that each option scored very low. Martha felt dispirited, worried that no job would truly satisfy her. When I asked her what kind of job would satisfy her most highly weighted factors such as taking advantage of her natural talents, providing opportunities to help people in the moment, and being active and on her feet, she finally uncorked the true desire that she'd kept buried for years beneath a pile of "shoulds." In her heart of hearts, she'd always wanted to be a nurse. However, the few times she'd confided this desire to someone, they told her she'd have more success as an executive. But after completing this exercise, her true career passion was undeniable. Her heart was pulling her hard toward nursing even though her head told her it would be costly to go back to school and difficult to let go of the prestige of her management career.

But once Martha put nursing on the table for consideration, we were able to address her concerns one by one. There was a way to marry her heart's desire with her head's abilities to have it all—eventually. There are numerous leadership roles available within the nursing field that could provide rich career opportunities down the road. While she pursues that long-term goal, she is enjoying her volunteer work in a nearby emergency department where she confirms each day that working in a hospital is the place for her. No prestigious management job or huge paycheck could give her more satisfaction than she receives from her patients' grateful smiles when she provides comfort just when they need it most.

The intangible parts of a job—autonomy, collegiality, prestige, purpose—can make an even bigger impact on our overall well-being than the easy-to-count factors like salary, benefits, and vacation time. To avoid undercounting the "soft" factors, try translating them into hard numbers. The way they add up might surprise you.

———————

Allison Rimm is a management consultant, speaker, and executive coach. She is the former senior vice president for strategic planning and information management at Massachusetts General Hospital and the author of *The Joy of Strategy: A Business Plan for Life* (Routledge, 2015).

CHAPTER 16

How to Build Expertise in a New Field

by Dorothy Leonard

Better pay, more joy on the job, or prerequisite to promotion? Whatever your reasons for deciding to build expertise in a new field, the question is how to get there.

Your goal, of course, is to become a swift and wise decision maker in this new arena, able to diagnose problems and assess opportunities in multiple contexts. You want what I call "deep smarts"—business critical, experience-based knowledge. Typically, deep smarts take years to develop; they're hard earned. But that doesn't mean it's too late for you to move into a different field.

Adapted from content posted on hbr.org, April 8, 2015 (product #H01ZF3).

The following steps can accelerate your acquisition of the expertise you need.

- **Identify the best exemplars.** Who is really good at what you want to do? Which experts are held in high regard by their peers and immediate supervisors? Whom do you want to emulate?

- **Assess the gap between them and you.** This requires brutal self-assessment. How much work will this change require, and are you ready to take it on? If you discover that the knowledge gap is fairly narrow, you should feel more confidence. If you determine that it's really wide, take a deep breath, and consider whether you have the courage and resolve to bridge it.

- **Study on your own.** Especially if the knowledge gap between you and experts in the new arena is wide, think about what you can do on your own to begin to narrow it. Self-study, talking to knowledgeable colleagues, and taking some online courses will help.

- **Persuade experts to share.** Many of them will be pleased to do so—especially if you've done your homework and have some foundational knowledge. But some may resist for a host of possible reasons, ranging from a lack of time to fear that you are after their job. Their reactions will depend heavily on both their personality and organizational culture. Strengthen your case by focusing on how helping you will benefit them. Perhaps you could take over some routine tasks that are tiresome to them but new to you. If the expert is a part of your own organization, management may reward any investment they make in developing talent. Emphasize that the time commitment can be minimal; you'll find short time slots in which to query them.

- **Learn to pull knowledge.** Become some combination of a bird of prey and a sponge—eagle-eyed for opportunities to learn and avid to absorb. Don't assume experts will tell you their most critical know-how in bullet points. That's impossible (because they know what they know in context, when it's called upon), insulting (because if it were that easy to impart, their knowledge wouldn't be worth much), and frustrating for you both (because lectures about how to do something rarely translate into true learning). Instead, use the two most powerful questions in eliciting knowledge: "Why?" and "Can you give me an example?"

- **Observe experts in action.** Concentrated observation is often more effective than interviews because it shows you how a person thinks and acts in real time. Ask to sit in on crucial meetings, accompany them to conferences and customer visits, and follow them as they solve problems. This is far from a passive process; you'll constantly need to ask yourself: Why did they do that? What was the effect? Would I have done it differently? Afterward, ask for a few minutes to debrief—even if it's just during a walk to the parking lot. Check what you observed against the expert's intention, and see if you can "teach it back" by explaining the steps taken and the reasons for them.

- **Seek mini experiences.** The next step is to identify opportunities to experience the environments, situations, or roles that have made the expert so valuable to the organization. Perhaps you can't go to medical school before becoming an MRI-machine designer like the person you're shadowing, but you can spend a week in a doctor's office. Maybe you didn't start out in your company's call center like the super sales manager you're emulating, but you could certainly work the telephones for a few days. Any "mini experience" that gives you a taste of the expert's much deeper understanding of a context that informs their judgment will help you gain insights. If nothing else, you will be equipped to ask better questions and pull knowledge more effectively.

- **Add visible value as soon as possible.** The experts and your new or future bosses will want to see some evidence that all this work is paying off. A log of what you have done and learned shows effort and progress. But if you can actually take over some small parts of an expert's job that they are willing (or eager) to relinquish—even better. Perhaps you can attend a conference or association meeting, teach part of an in-house course, or draft a report.

Developing expertise takes time. Estimates usually range from seven years or more. But if you follow the steps I've suggested here, you will have deep smarts—and be able to use them—much sooner.

———————

Dorothy Leonard is the William J. Abernathy Professor of Business Administration Emerita at Harvard Business School and chief adviser of the consulting firm Leonard-Barton Group. She is the author or coauthor of four Harvard Business Review Press books, including *Critical Knowledge Transfer* (2015).

SECTION FIVE

Get Inspired

Career change is possible. Read the stories in this section to hear from folks who've been sitting where you are now, who made the move, and who have found careers that addressed their needs for challenge, satisfaction, meaning, and fulfillment.

CHAPTER 17

Why You Should Have (at Least) Two Careers at the Same Time

by Kabir Sehgal

It's not uncommon to meet a lawyer who'd like to work in renewable energy, an app developer who'd like to write a novel, or an editor who fantasizes about becoming a landscape designer. Maybe you, too, dream about switching to a career that's drastically different from your current one. But you don't actually make the leap for a variety of reasons.

Adapted from content posted on hbr.org, April 25, 2017 (product #H03M9A).

The answer isn't to plug away at your current job. I think the answer is to *do both*. Two careers are better than one. And by committing to two careers, you'll experience the benefits of both.

In my case, I have four vocations: I'm a corporate strategist at a *Fortune* 500 company, a U.S. Navy Reserve officer, the author of several books, and a record producer. The two questions that people ask me most frequently are, "How much do you sleep?" and "How do you find time to do it all?" (My answers: "plenty," and "I make the time"). Yet these "process" questions don't get to the heart of my reasons and motivations. Instead, a more revealing query would be, "Why do you have multiple careers?" And the answer is that working many jobs makes me happier and leaves me more fulfilled. It also helps me perform better at each one. Here's how.

Subsidize Your Skill Development

My corporate job paycheck subsidizes my record-producing career. With no track record as a producer, nobody was going to pay me to produce their music, and it wasn't money that motivated me to become a producer in the first place—it was my passion for jazz and classical music. I volunteered to gain experience in this new industry. My day job not only afforded me the capital to make albums, but it also taught me the skills to succeed as a producer. A good producer should be someone who knows how to create a vision, recruit personnel, establish a timeline, raise money, and deliver products. After producing more than a dozen albums and winning a few Grammys, record labels and musicians started to reach out to see if they could hire me. I still refuse payment because making music, something that is everlasting, is reward enough for me.

At the same time, I typically invite my corporate clients to recording sessions. For someone who works at an office all day, it's exciting to go behind the scenes and interact with singers, musicians, and other creative professionals. While I was in Cuba making an album, one of my clients observed about the dancing musicians, "I've never been around people who have so much fun at work." That my corporate clients have a phenomenal experience only helps drive revenue at work, so my corporate and recording careers are mutually beneficial.

Make Friends in Different Circles

When I worked on Wall Street, my professional circle was initially limited to other folks in the financial services sector: bankers, traders, analysts, and economists. Taken together, all of us establish a "consensus" view on the markets. And most of my asset manager clients were looking for something different: "Give me a contrarian perspective." They didn't want to hear the groupthink. I took this as marching orders to search my rolodex for people who could provide my clients with a differentiated perspective.

For example, one of my clients wanted to understand what Chinese citizens were saying to each other. Because I am an author, I have gotten to know other writers, so I reached out to my friend who was a journalist at a periodical that monitors chatter in China. Not restricted (as I was) by the compliance department of a bank, he was able to give an unbridled perspective to my client, who was most appreciative. My client got a new idea. I got a trade. My friend got a new subscriber. By being in different circles, you can selectively introduce people who would typically never meet and add something for everyone.

Discover Real Innovations

When you work different jobs, you can identify where ideas interact—and more significantly, where they *should* interact. "It's technology married with liberal arts married with the humanities that yields us the result that makes our heart sing," said Steve Jobs, who was the embodiment of interdisciplinary thinking.

After Hurricane Katrina, many musicians left New Orleans. I wanted to help them. I could have created a typical nonprofit organization that solicits people for money. Instead, I helped create a more sustainable solution: a brokerage for musicians that I described as Wall Street meets Bourbon Street. People wanting to book a musician for a party in New York could find a band on my organization's website, which would then ask the booker to add a "tip" that would be allocated to a New Orleans–based charity. The booker (who in some cases was my corporate client) easily found a band for the party, the New York City–based musician got a gig, and the charity in New Orleans got a small donation. Because of my time working at a bank, I was able to create a different type of organization, one that has since merged with an even larger charitable organization.

When you follow your curiosities, you bring passion to your new careers and feel more fulfilled. And by doing more than one job, you may end up doing all of them better.

———————

Kabir Sehgal works in corporate strategy at a *Fortune* 500 company and previously served as a vice president at J.P. Morgan. He is also a U.S. Navy veteran and multiple Grammy- and Latin Grammy Award–winning record producer. He is the author of seven books, including *Coined: The Rich Life of Money and How Its History Has Shaped Us* (Grand Central Publishing, 2015).

CHAPTER 18

Advice from a Serial Life Reinventor: An Interview with Nilofer Merchant

by Sarah Green Carmichael

Most of us have some crazy dream living inside of us—start a company, write a book, move to Bali. Any of the above. All of the above. Maybe your dream is so crazy you haven't told anyone about it. Or maybe it's the thing you talk about every time you've had a bad day at the office. But what would it be like to actually chase down

Adapted from content posted on hbr.org, April 2, 2015 (product #H01ZD6).

that dream? I wanted to know. So I called former CEO and regular HBR contributor Nilofer Merchant.

Last year, Merchant fulfilled a dream when she packed up everything—her house, husband, and kid—and moved to Paris, where she planned to stay for at least a year, maybe more. It's not the first time she's radically reinvented her life. For instance, she's pivoted from being an executive in charge of billions of dollars worth of product at major tech companies like Apple and Autodesk to founding her own consulting firm—which she then shut down at the peak of its success. Her book *11 Rules for Creating Value in the Social Era* was named a Best Business Book of 2012 by *Fast Company* magazine, she gave an acclaimed TED talk, and she was given the Thinkers50 Future Thinker award in 2013. And then . . . Paris. I asked her how she decided to blow up her life midcareer—again—and make the leap. What follows is an edited version of our conversation.

HBR: What was the decision-making process like?

It started with a glass of wine. My husband and I talked about "crazy dreams." That night we probably generated 20 ideas, and I don't remember any of them except the one that stuck, which was "We should live a year abroad and give our son that experience." That was five years ago, and then three years ago we asked ourselves, "Are we serious? Because if we are, we should start." I would send him articles on Shanghai or Delhi and ask, "What about this? Or this?" In the end, choosing Paris was us coming to terms with the fact that it was going to be hard enough for all of us to relocate, but we thought it might not be quite as hard in Paris.

We also had to decide, Did our son (who was 10 years old at the time) get a vote? We've raised him to be involved in every decision. But we were also sure that if he had a vote, it would be a veto. We decided he would get to vote on where to live in the city and which school he got to go to, but we told him he couldn't vote on us doing it. Living abroad teaches you a bunch of skills and attributes you can't find in a textbook. That's the investment we're making in our son's life. We did it for him more than for us. Divergent thinking and creativity come from making a new map in your mind, and when you go to a new country, you build new cognitive maps. Once you've learned to have a new and different map, you can make more of them; your ability to adjust to one situation teaches you how to adjust to others.

What did you end up doing about your jobs?

My husband really didn't want to quit his job. So, he actually wrote a script, and he practiced the script ahead of time, and went into work a year out from the date we'd planned to move and said, "My family would like to move abroad. Is there any way I can move my job?" In the end, it took my husband's company nine months to say yes, to help us with the visa, but even toward the end, we were really starting to wonder what would happen.

You're a keynote speaker and someone who travels a lot for work anyway, so I would assume that your job was a lot more flexible and would be easy to move. Is that true?

Well . . . it wasn't seamless. It's costing me more in terms of travel time [to speaking engagements], so I'm doing fewer. But I've been able to add a European speaker's bureau, which is a positive. There have been other complications, too. I passed up a plum opportunity to be on a *Fortune* 100 board. Based on the time zones, I would have had to be on conference calls at 2 a.m. And when I thought about it, I realized that *this* priority of our family bucket list overruled my individual, professional bucket list. I had to tell myself to have faith that opportunities do come back around.

How did the reality of moving to another country match up with your expectations?

I hated the first six months for a variety of reasons. My son was really sad. He's in a foreign country and can't even do the homework assignment because he can't understand what it even *is*. We didn't insulate him by putting him in an American school or international school but in a full-on French school. So, it was hard to watch him be so sad. My husband was traveling for work probably 70% of the time for the first three to four months. And I felt like an idiot in every social interaction because my French was so bad. I went from being an effective communicator and competent person to just feeling stupid. So I questioned the decision, [but] this is how you learn and grow. It's not by having something be supereasy.

Was there a turning point?

There's no one moment; it's more that your shoulders come down from around your ears. I learned to laugh at myself a little more. My husband had to learn to say no a few more times at work. My son is now number two in his class in French when he is the only non-native speaker in his school. It's a truth that everyone loves the idea of what change gets you, but no one actually likes to change. And of course, we know it's a big privilege to be in a position to do this at all.

What would you say to other people who dream of changing countries midcareer?

Three things. First, it took five years for us to go from idea to reality. I think most people give themselves less runway and then wonder why it's so impossible. I see this same dynamic play out all the time in companies trying to change or innovate. It's like, "Let's cram for it like an exam" instead of building a set of practices that lets you make any idea into a new reality. Give yourself more time than you think you'll need.

I also think it was important that we said we would stay for at least a year. We'd heard enough stories from people who in the first three to six months just turned around and came home. But in our case, the commitment we made kept us working through the tough times.

Finally, we had to come to terms with the expense. Relocation is expensive anyway, and when we first moved, the dollar was $1.38 to the euro, and well, everything I bought I just wanted to cry. I finally said, this is just the expense of becoming more global. And that's worth a certain amount. Even if it doesn't financially make sense in terms of every single penny, it makes sense in terms of the bigger picture—in terms of what you're getting in return.

This isn't the first time you've radically changed your life or career. Does it get easier to embrace big, bold changes with practice?

This is the third major reinvention. And I will say that in each iteration, when you actually start, you feel like your success years are behind you. And then, three or five years later, you're like, "This was brilliant!" Not because it was obvious it would work out. But because in chasing the dream, you manifest this other thing: invention, reinvention, achievement. It is in the doing, you become.

As you begin that transformation process, you're tearing down the house you know to build the new house. Sure, you'll reuse some of the materials. But the tearing-down process is so scary because a part of you thinks, "What if I can't build it back up?" I think that's why most people don't do major change: because the teardown feels scary, and vulnerable, and destabilizing.

So are the internal challenges actually more pressing, in a way, than the external ones?

They're hard to separate. For instance, one day I went looking for index cards and five hours later I came back—without index cards—and lay on the couch and said, "I want to go home." So first it's thinking, "What are index cards called?" and figuring that out. Then it's going store by store through the neighborhood asking, in my terrible French, if they have this thing. And they don't. At home, it's just, "Oh, I need index cards." Go on Amazon. Click. And it's there the next morning. In France, Amazon doesn't quite work that way . . . stuff arrives when it wants to arrive. So after this five-hour hunt, I'm sprawled on the couch, defeated.

So some of that, clearly, is internal. But the external challenge was there. You're learning a bunch of things, and you learn first by not knowing. So any major change involves you feeling inadequate.

Looking back, any last advice?

The way you make your dreams come true? By making them come true.

———————

Sarah Green Carmichael is an executive editor at *Harvard Business Review*. **Nilofer Merchant** has personally launched 100 products amounting to $18 billion in revenue, and has served on both public and private boards. Today, she lectures at Stanford, gives talks around the world, and has been ranked one of the most influential management thinkers in the world by Thinkers50. Her latest book is *The Power of Onlyness: Make Your Wild Ideas Mighty Enough to Dent the World* (Viking, 2017).

CHAPTER 19

From Accountant to Yogi: Making a Radical Career Change

by Vijay Govindarajan and Hylke Faber

At some point, nearly all of us will experience a period of radical professional change. Some of us will seek it out; for others it will feel like an unwelcome intrusion into an otherwise stable career. Either way, we have choices about how we respond to it when it comes.

We recently caught up with yoga entrepreneur Leah Zaccaria, who put herself through the fire of change to completely reinvent herself. In her quest to live a life of

Adapted from content posted on hbr.org, May 23, 2016 (product #H02WMI).

purpose, the Seattle-based yogi shed her high-paying accounting job, her husband, and her home. In the process, she built a radically new life and career. Since then, she has founded two yoga studios, met a new life partner, and formed a new community of people.

Even if your personal reinvention is less drastic, we think there are lessons from her experience that apply.

Listen to the Whispers

Where do the seeds of change come from? The Cherokee have a saying: "Pay attention to the whispers so you won't have to hear the screams." Often the best ideas for big changes come from unexpected places—it's just a matter of tuning in. Great leaders recognize the weak signals or subtle signs that point to big changes to come. Leah reflects on a time she listened to the whispers: "About the time my daughter was five years old, I started having a sense that 'this isn't right.'" Leah realized that her life no longer matched her vision for it.

Up until that point in her life and career, Leah had followed traditional measures of success. After graduating with a degree in business and accounting, she joined a public accounting firm, married, bought a house, put lots of stuff in it, and had a baby. "I did what everybody else thought looked successful," she says. Leah easily could have fallen into a trap of complacency; instead, her restlessness sparked a period of experimentation and renewal.

Test the Future

Feeling the need for change, Leah started playing with future possibilities. She explored her interests and developed new capabilities. She first tried exercise and dieting and lost some weight and discovered an inner strength. "I felt empowered because I broke through my own limitations," she recalls.

However, it was another interest that led Leah to radically reinvent herself. "I remember sitting on a bench with my aunt at a yoga studio," she says, "and having an aha moment right then and there: Yoga is saving my life. Yoga is waking me up. I'm not happy and I want to change, and I'm done with this." In that moment of clarity Leah made an important leap, conquering her inner resistance to change and making a firm commitment. That clarity and resolve set her up to take bigger steps.

Practice Planned Opportunism

Creating the future you want is a lot easier if you are ready to capitalize on the opportunities that come your way. Simply put, we can practice "planned opportunism." When Leah made the commitment to change, she primed herself to new opportunities she may otherwise have overlooked. She recalls: "There was this coworker, Ryan, who has his office next to mine. One day, he said, 'Leah, let's go look at this space on Queen Anne.' He knew my love for yoga and had seen a space close to where he lived that he thought might be good to serve as a yoga studio. We went out there, and I was like, 'This is it, this is it! I've got to do it!' Of course I was scared, yet I had this strong sense of, 'I have to do this.'" Only a few months later, Leah opened her first yoga studio. But success was not instant.

Manage the Present, Shed the Past

Creating the future takes time. That's why leaders continue to manage the present while building toward the big nonlinear changes of the future. When it's time to make the leap, they take action and decisively drop what's no longer serving their purpose. Initially Leah stayed with her accounting job while starting up the yoga studio to make it all work. "I was working 60 hours a week and running a studio, so I wasn't getting very much sleep, but it was good for me," she says.

Soon after, she knew she had to make a bold move to fully commit to her new future. Within two years, Leah shed the safety of her accounting job and made the switch complete. Such drastic change is not easy.

Nourish Your Roots—Stay Connected to Your Purpose

"Be yourself," Leah says. "Quit being the person people think you're supposed to be. Find a way to dig deep into your courageous self to be who you are. Whatever that means as far as exploring your emotions, your identity, and your profession, find one version of you that you are always and everywhere."

Leah's sense of clarity for her purpose was sparked when she was 16 years old. "I was always a passionate person," she says. "One day I was at a party where I met this sage, a very energetic person called Christine. She and I get talking and then she stops, looks me in the eyes, and says—tears streaming down her face—'You are going to help a lot of people in this life. You are going to make a big difference.' That stuck with me forever." It was this sense of purpose that would carry Leah through the storms of change.

Be Resilient

Navigating change and facing obstacles brings us face-to-face with our fears. Leah reflects on one incident that triggered her anxiety, when her investors threatened to shut her down: "I was probably up against the most fear I've ever had," she says. "I had spent two years cultivating this community, and it had become successful very fast, within six months, and I was facing the prospect of losing it all."

She connected with her sense of purpose and dug deep, cultivating a tremendous sense of resilience. "I was feeling so intentional and strong that I wasn't going to let fear just take over. I was thinking, 'OK, guys, if you want to try to shut me down, shut me down.' And I knew it was a negotiation tactic, so I was able to say to myself, 'This is not real.'" By naming her fears and facing them head-on, Leah gained confidence. For most of us, letting go of the safety and security of the past gives us great trepidation. Calling out our concerns explicitly, as Leah did, can help us act decisively.

By letting go of her fears, Leah grew tremendously. "I learned that no matter what, I was going to be OK," she says. "Even if they shut me down, I've grown so much, I have been through so much, and my life has changed completely. I left my husband and went from a big house to couch hopping and staying in the basement of someone I met on Craigslist, of all things. I saw that I already had lost everything and I was fine."

See the Endless Cycle of Renewal

The cycle of renewal never ends. Leah's growth spurred her to open a second yoga studio—and it wasn't for the money. "I have no desire to make millions of dollars—it's not about that," she says. "It's about growth for me. Honestly, I didn't need to open a second studio. I had one, and it was highly successful. I was making as much money as I had as an accountant. But I know that if you don't grow, you stand still, and that doesn't work for me. I am here to grow and to help others grow. I want to inspire people to be better, to dig deep into their courageous self."

Consider the current moment in your own life, team, or organization. Where are you in the cycle of renewal: selectively forgetting the past, actively preserving the present, or boldly creating the future? What sage advice would Leah give you to move you ahead on your journey?

Wherever you are now, once you're on the path of growth, you can continually move through the seasons of transformation and renewal.

————————

Vijay Govindarajan is the Coxe Distinguished Professor at Dartmouth's Tuck School of Business and a Marvin Bower Fellow at Harvard Business School. He is the author of *The Three-Box Solution: A Strategy for Leading Innovation* (Harvard Business Review Press, April 2016). **Hylke Faber** is the author of *Taming Your*

Crocodiles: Unlearn Fear and Become a True Leader (Ixia Press, 2018). He leads the coaching and facilitation organizations Constancee and the Growth Leaders Network, and serves as faculty director for the Columbia Business School Executive Education Leader as Coach programs.

Index

reawakening passion for, 7–29
See also career; job
working identity, 90, 93, 97–98,
103–110, 111
work-life balance, 12–13, 43,
77, 78

work situation, assessing current,
42–43

Zaccaria, Leah, 185–191

Smart advice and inspiration from a source you trust.

If you enjoyed this book and want more comprehensive guidance on essential professional skills, turn to the HBR Guides Boxed Set. Packed with the practical advice you need to succeed, this seven-volume collection provides smart answers to your most pressing work challenges, from writing more effective emails and delivering persuasive presentations to setting priorities and managing up and across.

Harvard Business Review Guides

Available in paperback or ebook format. Plus, find downloadable tools and templates to help you get started.

- Better Business Writing
- Building Your Business Case
- Buying a Small Business
- Coaching Employees
- Delivering Effective Feedback
- Finance Basics for Managers
- Getting the Mentoring You Need
- Getting the Right Work Done

- Leading Teams
- Making Every Meeting Matter
- Managing Stress at Work
- Managing Up and Across
- Negotiating
- Office Politics
- Persuasive Presentations
- Project Management

HBR.ORG/GUIDES

Buy for your team, clients, or event.
Visit hbr.org/bulksales for quantity discount rates.

Notes

Notes

Notes

Notes

Notes

Notes

Notes

Notes

Notes

Notes

Notes

Notes